25 Years of Innovation: The Story of Pfizer Central Research

By Ogden Tanner

GREENWICH PUBLISHING GROUP, INC.
LYME, CONNECTICUT

PRODUCED AND PUBLISHED BY

Greenwich Publishing Group, Inc.
Lyme, Connecticut

Design by Bill Brown Design

Separation & film assembly by Silver Eagle Graphics, Inc.

PHOTOGRAPHY CREDITS

p. 4	Timothy Behl
p. 110	Pete Saloutos The Stock Market 1992
p. 117	Jose L. Pelaez The Stock Market 1992
p. 120-121	Pete Saloutos The Stock Market 1995

All other photographs courtesy of Pfizer Central Research
Division and Pfizer Inc.

Library of Congress Catalog Card Number: 95-82399
ISBN: 0-944641-17-2
First Printing: March 1996
10 9 8 7 6 5 4 3 2 1

TABLE OF CONTENTS

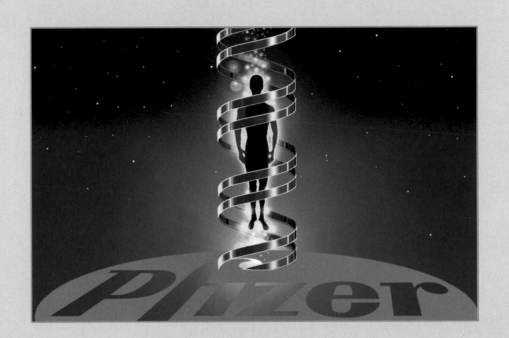

I joined Pfizer in 1967, and Central Research and I grew up together. During those years, I read Sam Mines' *An Informal History of Pfizer* and got a kick out of hearing about the small, informal, fermentation-centered research atmosphere in the pre-Central Research era, that led to Pfizer's early commercial successes in specialty chemicals and antibiotics.

With the creation of the Central Research Division in 1971, Pfizer research changed dramatically. Research would become big, broadly targeted, systematized and carefully managed. Many of today's (and yesterday's) technical management consultants might have predicted that this new organizational style would surely spell the end of Pfizer creativity and productivity. They would, obviously, have guessed very wrong. We got big, but the entrepreneurial, can-do spirit never died.

I wanted our new generation of Central Research employees to have a feel for those 25 years of transition, growth, maturation and outstanding productivity. Hence, this book.

The creation of the book itself was to be a relatively simple project: hire a professional writer, let him interview a number of researchers who had lived the history and then write the story. I was to relearn something you'd have thought I would know by now. Nothing is simple.

In the end, the book was created by many authors and editors. They took the ball far down the field, but it would never have crossed the goal line without the patient, careful efforts of the man who's quarterbacked so many games for me, Joe Lombardino. Thanks for another one, Joe.

So, Pfizer research colleagues, read and enjoy learning about your heritage. Twenty-five years from now, when the second edition comes out, the structure of Pfizer research will almost certainly have evolved far from its 1996 configuration. But I'll bet it's still viewed as one of the toughest, most respected and most productive applied research operations in the world.

JOHN F. NIBLACK

January 1996

1

The Coming Revolution

A scientist at Pfizer Central Research, Groton, Connecticut, studies a backlighted pattern involved in gene sequencing. This new field has launched the company on a "spectacular voyage of discovery" aimed at the invention of new drugs.

At Pfizer today, there is excitement in the air.

Like his colleagues, Executive Vice President for Research and Development John Niblack knows the significance of the threshold on which the pharmaceutical industry is poised. He talks about the research breakthroughs that have opened the door to a world of new drugs.

"Today we can select any disease target that we choose," says Niblack, "and by attacking it from the genes backwards, we can select new targets, new approaches, and move into those areas at will. We can do so on a prospective basis; the tools of molecular genetics permit us to move forward in areas where we feel it would be most advantageous to innovate."

"We are entering a golden age of therapeutic innovation," says Barry Bloom, Niblack's predecessor, who stepped down in 1993 after 22 years at the helm of Pfizer's R&D.

"It's now possible to do things that weren't doable before, and possible to do things with a speed that was unheard of in the past," says Bloom. "We are entering a stage in which we will see the emergence of an unparalleled number and kind of experimental drugs.

"New techniques in the field of molecular genetics now make it possible to create in a test tube exact clones of human cellular structures that have potential significance as targets for drugs. Furthermore, through use of a miniaturized robotic system to test compounds for their affinity for the target, we can move at a mind-boggling rate. At Pfizer, for example, we can run through a library of 300,000 compounds in a matter of months. We've got better abilities to screen and computers to process all the data. The whole thing adds up to a power, a leverage, a capability, that's just unprecedented.

"This revolutionary capability applies to the industry as a whole, but we have some proprietary techniques, some trade secrets, particularly in this area of high-speed screening, that have given us a competitive

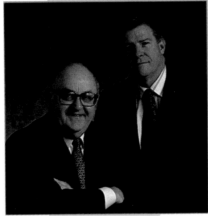

Pfizer's executive vice president for Research and Development, John Niblack, right, is shown with Barry Bloom, his predecessor. Says Bloom of the future of Central Research: "We are entering a golden age of therapeutic innovation [in which] we will see the emergence of an unparalleled number of new drugs."

edge. Eventually that edge will disappear, as is always the case in industrial competition. But for the moment, at least, we're very pleased to be somewhat ahead of the pack."

One area of research racing forward at great speed, with fantastic prospects for human health, is the rapidly expanding knowledge of genetic structure. George Milne, who succeeded Niblack as president of Central Research, outlines the significance of this new frontier in medicine:

"One seminal example shows what's so striking about the period we're entering. You've got roughly 100,000 genes in your body, and in the last 17 years the structures of about 4,000 of those genes have been determined. In the next five years we will essentially know the structures of *all* the genes in the human body. Once that happens, we can think about whole new kinds of therapeutic interventions – you will actually have the ability to implant a gene in people who are deficient in it and, hence, cure a disease."

Says Alan Proctor, Pfizer's former executive director of Molecular Genetics and Protein Chemistry, now executive director of Immunology and Infectious

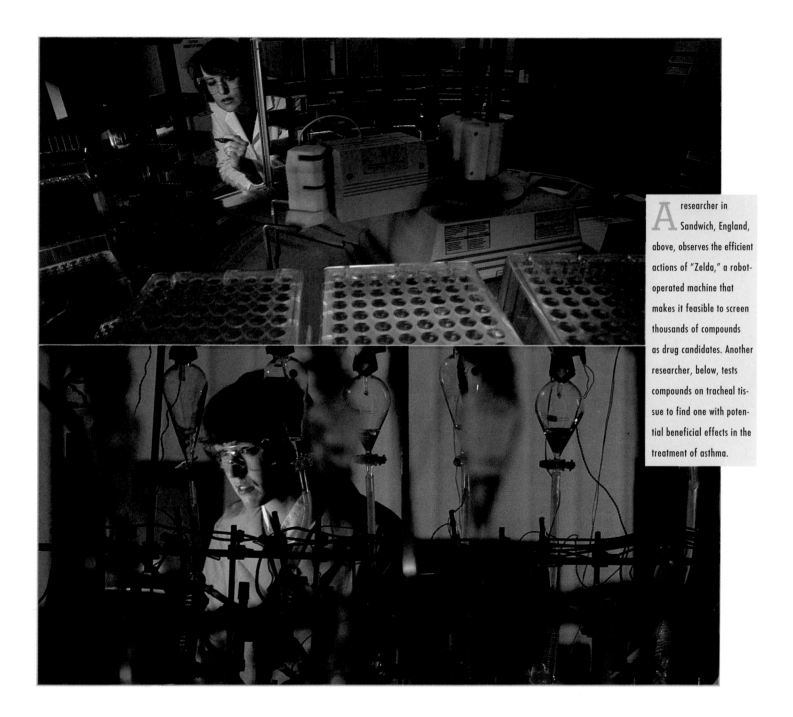

A researcher in Sandwich, England, above, observes the efficient actions of "Zelda," a robot-operated machine that makes it feasible to screen thousands of compounds as drug candidates. Another researcher, below, tests compounds on tracheal tissue to find one with potential beneficial effects in the treatment of asthma.

a Nobel laureate in chemistry. When the two were seniors, they did their undergraduate thesis together (on a chemical process called the Diel's-Alder Reaction). Later, at MIT's graduate school, Bloom met a young man named Gerald Laubach, who had come there from the University of Pennsylvania and was assigned to the same lab.

Laubach, Bloom and Corey all worked for Professor John Sheehan, who had spent the war years with Merck, Sharp & Dohme and later was to become famous for his penicillin synthesis research. Because their classmates included a number of industrial chemists from Merck who returned after the war to earn advanced degrees, they remember being surrounded by people who were not only accomplished laboratory scientists but had also developed a practical, mission-oriented attitude toward research.

After MIT, Bloom took a year of postdoctoral training on a National Research Council fellowship at the University of Wisconsin, where he worked on steroid synthesis. His decision to come to Pfizer in 1952 as a research chemist was largely due to Laubach, who had already joined Pfizer and whom Bloom regarded highly. Laubach and Bloom were to work together for al-

most 40 years, until the former retired in 1991.

In the early 1950s, while he worked at the old Brooklyn plant, Bloom satisfied his passion for music, attending chamber music concerts in New York City and standing at the rear of the Metropolitan Opera for a dollar. (Until he gave it up, he played the trombone, for the Sanford, Maine, town concert band and later for the MIT dance band.) Those were also the years of the so-

Barry Bloom

Barry Bloom was already moving towards his future career when he was around 11 or 12 years old. "I was mad for chemistry." He recalls that he, "had a chemistry set and a little laboratory in the basement, where I used to play for hours on end."

Bloom was born in Roxbury, Massachusetts. After he graduated from high school in June 1945, he went right on to the Massachusetts Institute of Technology in July. "There were no scientists in my family," he says. "But I did have one uncle who went to MIT, in the class of 1918, and with the clarity of youth, I saw him as a symbol of what I would really like to do. I knew I wanted to go to MIT; it was as simple as that."

At college, he was a contemporary and close friend of E. J. Corey, who later became

called Jackson Heights Boys Club, named after a group of young bachelors who worked for Pfizer and who shared an apartment in Queens – Bloom, Laubach, Rex Pinson, Bob Feeney and Eugene Agnello.

"We were pretty unexciting types," confesses Bloom. "They used to make fun of me, claiming that I spent all my time reading *Chemical Abstracts* while they did the cooking and the dish washing. That's about as wild a joke as you could make about that crowd."

The bachelors, however, with the exception of Feeney, were all outdoor enthusiasts, and they used to go skiing on weekends in Vermont – in those days a seven- or eight-hour drive. One day, they spotted an ad for a well-worn 1939 Packard hearse that an undertaker in Yonkers was willing to part with for $200. They chipped in and bought it, removing the machinery for sliding caskets and replacing it with four bunk beds made of stretched canvas. For several years, the Boys Club had ideal sleep-in transportation. When it came time to get rid of the hearse, they decided to give it to the MIT Outing Club. Months later, someone sent them a clipping from the *Boston Globe* about a couple of MIT students receiving a summons for sleeping in the street in an automobile – which turned out to be their old hearse.

Bloom played a major role in discovering an antidepressant drug called Niamid, which was marketed in 1964. In 1967, the central nervous system group that he headed also produced Navane, a drug for schizophrenia, and in 1969, Sinequan, another antidepressant.

From there, the ladder of promotion reached steadily upward. In 1968, Bloom was made director of Medicinal Products Research and Development. In 1971, he became president of the Central Research Division and vice president for Research, and in 1992, he was promoted to executive vice president for Research and Development.

Of all his contributions to Central Research, Bloom feels that the most significant was the fact that he recruited good people; many of today's senior Central Research

managers are persons whom he helped hire. People, he emphasizes, are the critical factor in the success of any organization.

Secondly, he helped create the mission-oriented culture that prevails in Central Research. "Scientists needed to be made to understand that industrial research differed from the academic research they were accustomed to conducting for their Ph.D. theses," he says. Industrial research, he taught, involves good science applied to business needs – a focusing of science in order to find new medicinals for Pfizer to bring to the medical community and the patient.

H ead of Central Research since its inception in 1971 until 1990, Barry Bloom shaped this division as no other did and prepared it to face the future.

Lastly, Bloom brought both the operations at Sandwich and Amboise to a healthy, productive state. Through the people he appointed and supervised, such as Lloyd Conover, both organizations were turned around to become the highly successful, excellent research centers they are today.

After 41 illustrious years with the company, Barry Bloom retired as Pfizer's executive vice president for Research and Development in 1993.

Diseases: "The thing that's so exciting is that genetic causes of diseases are being discovered on a daily basis. Within the next five years, every bit of the 3 billion bits of DNA in our bodies is going to be isolated and sequenced. The whole book of the chemistry of our bodies is going to be written in the next five years.

"Automated DNA sequencing has thrust us upon a spectacular voyage of discovery. The resulting explosion of information will present a unique opportunity for the prepared pharmaceutical company. We're tremendously excited about meeting the challenge which the coming 'decade of the gene' will present."

Pfizer, says Milne, is not only prepared, but positioned to lead the industry into this promising and challenging future.

"We're going to come out of the next five years broadly recognized as one of the leading pharmaceutical companies in the country, if not the outright leader," he says. "There's no question that we have one of the richest, if not the richest, drug pipelines in the industry. Our scientists are at least twice as productive as our competitors at discovering new medicines."

Central Research is the division of Pfizer that's at the center of the action in the current revolution, and it's responsible for keeping the development "pipeline" full of potential new medicines. The company has received kudos from all sides as a result of this division's leadership in the search for new and better products. "Pfizer has the best product line of any drug company," says William F. Harnisch, president of Forstmann-Leff Associates Inc., an institutional investor.

Currently no fewer than 4,500 of Pfizer's 40,000 employees are engaged in research and development – about 2,500 in Groton, Connecticut; about 1,500 in Sandwich, England; and lesser numbers in Nagoya, Japan; Amboise, France; Terre Haute, Indiana; Lincoln, Nebraska; and New York City, where the company has additional R&D operations. These laboratories are organized under one management structure in Central Research, which helps to coordinate and focus their research efforts. The Groton laboratories specialize in research on therapies for diseases of the central nervous system, inflammatory diseases (such as arthritis), immunological disorders, cancer, diabetes, obesity, osteoporosis and bacterial diseases. Sandwich's primary focus is on drugs for cardiovascular diseases, but it also researches pulmonary diseases such as asthma, chronic bronchitis and allergic rhinitis along with infectious, viral, neurological, gastrointestinal and urogenital diseases. Nagoya concentrates mainly on inflammation and pain projects, looking for new, nonaddictive analgesics and novel ways of interfering with the inflammation process.

As each research center designs and synthesizes a new compound, a potential new medicine, it is given a code number with a prefix: CP ("Charles Pfizer") for those compounds originated in the United States; U.K. ("United Kingdom") for those developed in England; and CJ ("Central Research, Japan") for those invented in Japan.

There are also several other locations at which Pfizer has smaller research operations. In Amboise, France, the company has a research center in animal toxicology; in Terre Haute, Indiana, it maintains an experimental farm; in Lincoln, Nebraska, there are animal health research laboratories; and in New York City, where the company has its corporate headquarters, there is a Central Research Department of Clinical and Scientific Affairs.

The range of skills these 4,500 people represent is awesome. The scientists work not only with the traditional test tubes and petri dishes, but also with powerful computers and a host of other modern technologies, including robotic aids. To see them going about their tasks is an astounding, and somewhat humbling, experience.

In recent years, Pfizer has spent several billion dollars on research and development, most of it for pharmaceutical research. Since 1993, its research investment *each year* has topped $1 billion. R&D has paid off with the success of the following leading products discovered at Pfizer:

• Diflucan, the world's leading antifungal drug. Well tolerated and cost-effective, Diflucan enables physicians to make wider use of antifungal therapy, particularly in patients with suppressed immune systems — such as those with AIDS, cancer patients undergoing chemotherapy, organ transplant patients and burn victims — who are particularly susceptible to serious fungal infections. Pfizer's Patient Assistance Program provides Diflucan free of charge to needy patients, many of whom suffer from AIDS or are infected with HIV.

• Norvasc, a calcium channel blocker for treating angina and hypertension. This once-a-day treatment provides smooth control of blood pressure with minimal side effects. It provides constant control of blood pressure and is well tolerated, leading to high patient acceptance.

• Zoloft, a well-tolerated, once-a-day antidepressant launched in the U.S. in early 1992. This agent inhibits the cellular re-uptake of a brain amine known as serotonin, thus relieving depression. Zoloft is also undergoing review by the U.S. Food and Drug Administration for use in treating another serious illness, obsessive-compulsive disorder.

• Zithromax, a once-a-day oral antibiotic launched in the U.S. in early 1992. Zithromax provides "targeted delivery" of the drug to the infection site, resulting in a cure after only a five-day course of therapy. A single dose is sufficient to cure sexually transmitted chlamydia infections. Shorter courses of therapy result in a higher compliance rate – the patient is more inclined to take all of his medicine as directed.

• Cardura, a drug for hypertension. This agent lowers blood pressure by relaxing the arteries, providing excellent control with minimal side effects. Studies show that Cardura is also very effective in treating the urinary problems caused by enlarged prostates, a common problem in older men. The company carried out a clinical program to establish this indication and received approval for use in 1995.

• Tenidap, a mechanistically unusual once-a-day treatment for arthritis, has been filed with the FDA. This structurally unique agent has been shown in large clinical trials to influence certain key hormones, called cytokines, that are associated with the progression of arthritis. This property, together with its ability to reduce pain and swelling in the arthritic joint, makes tenidap the first drug of its type for treating arthritis.

• Glucotrol XL, a new formulation of Pfizer's antidiabetic compound glipizide, uses the extended-release, once-a-day Alza delivery system, for patient convenience.

In addition to drugs developed by Pfizer R&D, Procardia, a drug targeted for hypertension and angina, was licensed from the German firm Bayer in 1981. The

In a biotechnology laboratory in Groton, Connecticut, a research scientist works with a cell culture unit that produces mammalian cells used in identifying new drug leads.

most successful cardiovascular drug ever launched, it is currently the third-largest-selling pharmaceutical in the United States. Procardia XL, launched in 1989, controls angina and hypertension for up to 24 hours with a once-a-day dosage form licensed from the Alza Corporation.

However, a pharmaceutical company can't rely only on their drugs already in the marketplace, no matter how successful they are, and Pfizer has no intention of resting on past achievements. Its pipeline is bulging with new medications at various stages of development. Among them are:

• Dofetilide, a new class of drug that safely controls various types of abnormal heart rhythms. An antiarrhythmic compound that is a specific inhibitor of an ion channel in the heart, it is in the late stages of clinical development.

• Ziprasidone, a new therapy for psychotic illness with reduced side effects, is in Phase III of clinical development.

• Trovafloxacin, an antibiotic with a broad spectrum of activity, including successful treatment of some pneumonia-causing bacteria that are resistant to other antibiotics, is in late stages of development.

• Donepezil (E-2020), licensed from the Eisai company and now in registration, promises to be a well-tolerated drug for treating Alzheimer's disease.

Further down the road are dozens of compounds

that are targeted at almost every major affliction, including AIDS, stroke, atherosclerosis, cancer and osteoporosis.

Some of Pfizer's recent discoveries, such as one designated "substance P antagonist," mark the company as a creator of firsts – and illustrate how much time it can take to develop a new drug. Discovered in 1931, the structure of Substance P was finally determined in 1961. In the late 1980s, Pfizer scientists, using human receptors, high-speed robotics and other tools of molecular biology, were able to discover a molecule that blocks precisely the actions of substance P and fights pain – the first in the world. Concludes George Milne: "It is an example of Pfizer being out ahead of everyone else in the drug revolution, blazing the trails as an innovator."

Pfizer's current role in the drug revolution is recorded in a thick, loose-leaf book titled Pfizer Discovery Research Portfolio – Project OperatingPlans – Confidential.

The book covers over 100 separate projects that Pfizer is working on, each with a medical rationale, a business plan and a Discovery team of about five to nine scientists. Included is a wide range of therapeutics such as antibacterials, antivirals, antifungals, cardiovascular and gastrointestinal; treatments for atherosclerosis, cancer, diabetes, inflammation, neurodegenerative diseases, osteoporosis, pain, respiratory diseases and urogenital diseases; psychotherapeutics; and various other potential compounds being explored through molecular genetics and protein chemistry.

Says George Milne: "Our research is not unlike that of a first-class venture-capital firm. You don't know in advance which project is really going to be successful; any one can be Pfizer's next Feldene or Diflucan. The trick is to leave the ownership of each project, and the creativity and the incentive, at the project level while creating an environment that is challenging and at the same time encouraging."

Out of these projects have come several dozen compounds, from Central Research's laboratories in Groton, Sandwich and Nagoya, that are currently at some stage in the development pipeline. The prospects for these compounds illustrate another facet of today's drug industry: the increasing expense of finding new, safe, effective medicines.

Of the thousands of new compounds synthesized each year at Pfizer as potential new medicines, fewer than 20 will enter the development phase. Of the drugs currently in development, past experience predicts that only 1 out of 15 will make it – 93 percent will fall by the way. Only 7 percent will have the high levels of efficacy and safety necessary to bring a drug to market.

Whereas it took about $1 million for Pfizer to discover, develop and get approval for Terramycin in 1950, 1990 surveys of the pharmaceutical industry, using data from the early 1980s, revealed that it cost an average of $231 to $359 million to develop one successful drug, up from $54 million in 1976 and $125 million in 1987. Today the figure is believed to be in excess of $400 million.

While Terramycin took about one year from discovery to approval, today a drug spends an average of several years in the discovery process, plus about 10 years of development and registration time – some 13 to 20 years of endeavor from the time a scientist has an idea to the time when the drug actually hits the market. U.S. patents to protect a new drug are supposed to give a company 20 years of protection from the time of filing, but patents must be taken out so early in the research process that market exclusivity has been effectively cut to no more than 10 and as little as 6 years. It is during this relatively short period of exclusivity that the company must recoup the enormous research and development costs for the new drug, as well as the costs for all the many failed projects.

If a compound is rejected at any point in the process, it means millions of dollars down the drain.

Someone has to pay for the many failures, and all of that financing comes out of Pfizer's corporate-income stream. Still, as some pharmaceutical companies are now discovering, avoiding the risk of failure can be disastrous; many of those companies' pipelines have dried up.

"Failure's the name of the game," says Joseph Lombardino, senior director of Operations Planning. "You have to be patient in this business, and you have to take hope from the small technical successes that come along the way.

"We are investing about $1.5 billion a year in research," Lombardino continues. "That's a tremendous drain on the company unless we are able to discover, develop and launch a stream of products that earn us significant income. The problem is that the billion we're investing in early drug development today won't pay off in successful drugs until 2004 or later. A few of the good ideas our Discovery scientists have today may deliver drugs in 2009. You need some far-sighted management, with real risk-taking attributes and confidence in their R&D people, to play in this business."

"Far-sighted management." "An environment that is challenging and encouraging." Those phrases are heard again and again when Pfizer employees talk about their company. They indicate the major factors that have made Pfizer a research leader in the industry.

Drug research is surely one of the most scientifically exacting of human activities. To do it well requires people with prodigious knowledge and talent as well as an organization that can focus and coordinate the technical, managerial and regulatory complexities of their work. In Central Research, Pfizer has an operation that puts all the pieces together.

Timothy Subashi, a scientist in the Molecular Sciences Department in Groton, is just one of the many talented professionals dedicated to turning Pfizer's investment in research and development into ground breaking new drugs.

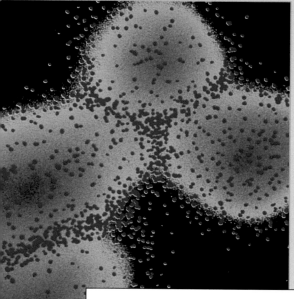

these, only one, on average, will actually reach the market.

A scientist intent on discovering a new medicine must first be aware of the worldwide knowledge base concerning the partic-

cost of more than $80 billion annually. Clearly there is a huge medical need. There are a number of alternative research approaches to Alzheimer's now being pursued. One is to replace lost mental capacity in the elderly using a drug that is safer than existing therapy. Another approach seeks to prevent the death of brain cells, which, along with improving memory, could provide ameliorative therapy for a large number of early-stage Alzheimer's sufferers. Yet another research

New Ideas for Treating Major

Once in a blue moon, a scientist stumbles on an idea for a new drug, or a new and unexpected use for an existing drug turns up in clinical use. But in the overwhelming majority of cases, research begins more systematically with a recognized medical need, which, in the prepared mind of the scientist, leads to an idea for meeting that need.

It is a long, painstaking process, according to Joe Lombardino, senior director of Operations Planning. From an idea for a new drug through research and development to product launch can take up to 20 years and cost over $400 million. Furthermore, it is highly risky. Of as many as 10,000 chemicals synthesized annually by a typical large pharmaceutical company, only 12 to 18 will become development candidates, and of

ular disease that the new medicine will ultimately treat. This knowledge base is constantly expanding as new findings come in from various sources such as the National Institutes of Health, academia and university hospitals and the pharmaceutical industry itself. From a variety of sources, including published materials and contacts with other scientists, the research scientist must integrate what is known about the disease, including whatever is known about the mechanism by which the disease is initiated and perpetuated, before he can apply his own experience and intuition to conceiving an idea for new therapy. And the diseases awaiting new therapy are many.

For example, *Alzheimer's disease* currently afflicts some 4 million Americans at a total

approach is understanding the basic physiology and biochemistry of Alzheimer's in an attempt to interrupt the disease at the cellular level. If the release of key mediators can be prevented, a true cure for Alzheimer's might be at hand. Unfortunately, this last approach involves the greatest research effort, with at least 10 years needed before results from human clinical trials can be expected.

AIDS is another area in which the pharmaceutical industry has invested heavily, with almost 100 ongoing research projects. There are a variety of ways to approach AIDS, including gene therapy, a vaccine, direct antiviral agents and modulation of the host immune system. Pharmaceutical companies have come together to share early successes in the Intercompany Collaboration on AIDS Drug Research, but the cure is still many years away, with a trail of failed projects already identifiable.

An estimated 10 million Americans suffer from *urinary incontinence*. Several approaches to this medical problem are being investigated that seek to avoid the side effects of current drugs, which include dry mouth, blurred vision and constipation. Receptor sub-types that affect cell function of smooth muscle in the bladder but not the heart are being iso-

ogy of the disease. A protein called amylin has been implicated as a possible underlying cause of diabetes. A drug that prevents the synthesis of amylin or inhibits its action could be a breakthrough therapy. In another approach, inhibitors of an enzyme called aldose reductase have shown promise in improving the nerve physiology and potentially preventing end-stage diabetic complications like blindness, kidney failure and cardiovascular disease. Several such enzyme in-

stop uncontrolled cell division and increasing the recognition of tumor cells by the body's immune system. All are being investigated but are many years away from practical, effective therapy.

Resistance to antibiotics for treatment of *infectious diseases* is increasing at an alarming rate. Resistant tuberculosis is a growing, serious problem. New, more effective antibiotics are needed quickly. There are a number of approaches under investigation

Diseases

lated and used to test potential new drugs.

Some 10 million American males are *impotent*. Current treatments are generally unsatisfactory, with surgical prostheses being quite costly. There is presently no approved drug therapy. Some approaches involve targeting tissue-specific inhibitors and directly influencing sexual mood by inhibiting chemicals implicated in controlling sexual function.

There are some 14 million *diabetic* Americans. Costs total nearly $100 billion annually, including hospitalization and treatment for cardiovascular disease and eye, nerve and kidney damage. One strategy is to reduce these complications with effective drugs that reduce blood sugar levels and that directly intervene in the pathophysiol-

hibitors are in late stages of development.

The U.S. industry association, called the Pharmaceutical Research and Manufacturers of America, has determined that there are more than 120 potential new medicines under development by pharmaceutical companies for the treatment of various types of *cancer*, whose direct and indirect costs are estimated at $100 billion annually in the United States. There have been some successes in treating childhood leukemia, Hodgkin's disease and testicular cancer, but clearly there is a need for better, new classes of anticancer drugs. Multiple therapies may be needed to achieve a cure. Some approaches include ways to tie up an oncogene to prevent its effects on cells, restoring the effects of a suppressor gene to

for overcoming bacterial resistance. One is to continue the well-precedented method of screening natural products for their antibacterial properties. Another is to find drugs that interfere with the spread of bacteria through the body. A third is to discover how bacteria evade drugs and interfere with their defenses. All of these approaches are under investigation.

Identifying a medical need is usually not too difficult. However, finding an effective drug to treat it is like finding a needle in a haystack. Pfizer Central Research continues in its endeavor to find quality new drugs that can meet these needs.

2

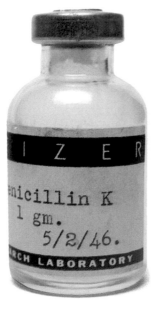

This early picture from the archives shows a Pfizer chemist working to refine the production of penicillin by fermentation. The company produced 90 percent of the penicillin that went ashore with the Allied Forces on the beaches of Normandy in June 1944.

CHAPTER TWO

A Company Reborn

For all its recent successes, Pfizer is a Johnny-come-lately in the pharmaceutical industry. It is probably the last major company to enter the drug business, but nevertheless, it has gone on to become one of the world's leading players.

Like many other technology-based American companies, Pfizer's destiny was strongly influenced by World War II. The business was started by Charles Pfizer and his cousin Charles Erhart as a small fine-chemicals factory in Brooklyn in 1849. Nearly a century later, in 1941, it was making citric acid on a large scale by fermentation. Britain, intrigued by the lifesaving properties of the recently identified antibiotic penicillin but under bombardment from Nazi Germany, had appealed to Washington for help, and U.S. companies rose to the challenge. Pfizer put its knowledge of fermentation technology to work, and on March 1, 1944, the first commercial plant for the large-scale production of penicillin was opened in a converted ice factory in Brooklyn. It cost $3 million to build — a big gamble for a company whose total revenues were $7 million that year. By using 10,000-gallon fermentation tanks, it was able to produce 90 percent of the penicillin that went ashore with the Allied Forces on the beaches of Normandy in June, 1944.

Even though it manufactured most of the penicillin supply, Pfizer was not then in the business of marketing its own drugs; it sold the penicillin in bulk to companies like Lilly, Parke-Davis and Upjohn, which then distributed the product under their own labels, with Pfizer's name appearing only in small print.

Then came a rude awakening. In those days, the pharmaceutical industry was comprised of two different types of companies: research and manufacturing companies and marketing and distribution companies. Rarely did any one company combine these different aspects of the business. The relative ease of producing large quantities of penicillin changed this scenario. Some of Pfizer's largest customers began to build their own

John E. McKeen examines a "ball-and-stick" model of a molecule in the 1960s. As superintendent of Pfizer's facility in Brooklyn, New York, he brought the first deep-tank penicillin plant into existence in less than four months in 1944. He served as company president from 1949 to 1965, and as chairman from 1950 to 1968.

fermentation plants and cancel their standing orders. Pfizer was left with many idle employees, heavy investment in manufacturing plants and large inventories of penicillin. Recovering from the shock and venturing into new territory, Pfizer started to put its own label on penicillin for sale to large hospitals and, to a lesser extent, overseas.

Spurred by the success of penicillin, many pharmaceutical companies with established research programs began searching for other new antibiotics, leaving Pfizer to face a critical decision. Up to that time, the company had never done research to discover new products of any kind. Research was a risky and expensive business, but Pfizer plunged in with a program to screen soil samples for undiscovered antibiotics, eventually testing some 135,000 samples from around the world, using trial-and-error methods that were then the norm.

To get the samples, Pfizer enlisted the aid of volunteers: travelers, missionaries, explorers, airline pilots, students, housewives and Pfizer sales agents. They were encouraged to pick up a teaspoon of earth, seal it in a packet and mail it to Brooklyn for a small reward. Soil came in from the jungles of Brazil, from the tops of

Penicillium, from which penicillin is extracted, is a colorful microorganism, left. Pfizer built upon its expertise in deep tank fermentation (which it employed in the production of citric acid) to become the first to successfully mass produce penicillin.

mountains and the bottoms of mine shafts, from cemeteries, from deserts, from the ocean; balloons were even sent up to collect soil that was airborne.

As each sample came in and was properly labeled as to its source, it was diluted with sterile water and put in a petri dish with a nutrient medium to see if a colony of mold would grow. If it did, a promising specimen was transplanted to a test tube filled with sterile agar medium. When a good-sized colony was growing, small discs of blotting paper were dipped in the solution and placed on petri dishes in which different bacteria had been seeded. If an antibiotic were present, it would inhibit the growth of bacteria around the disc, forming a clear ring. And if this looked promising, tests were car-

ried out by injecting the medium containing antibiotic into infected mice and guinea pigs. Dozens of potential antibiotics were discovered by such methods, but most were too toxic to be considered: they would kill disease germs, but they might kill the patient, too.

In 1949, exactly a century after Charles Pfizer sold his first product, in a laboratory at the same Brooklyn site, a yellow powder with strong antibiotic properties was isolated and labeled PA-76 — meaning "Pfizer Antibiotic." It was produced by a new soil organism, which Pfizer named *Streptomyces rimosus*. Generically, the compound is now known as oxytetracycline, and it proved both safe and effective against a range of bacteria that caused more than a hundred infectious diseases. The company named

a common laborer worked backbreaking hours for five dollars a week.

From the beginning, the cousins concentrated on quality and on chemicals not then produced in the United States, giving them a tariff advantage over imports. Pfizer had been an apothecary's apprentice and Erhart had learned the confectioner's trade. Not surprisingly, their first product, Santonin, combined the skills of each. Santonin was a compound extracted from the dried flower

winemaking — and turning them into tartar and tartaric acid used by bakers, beverage manufacturers and housewives. By 1871, sales had reached $1.4 million a year.

In 1880, in a move of major significance, Pfizer began using concentrated lemon juice imported from Italy to make citric acid and marketing it for use in medicinals, foods, soft drinks and candy. But as the world demand for lemons rose, growers could get a higher price selling the fruit as an edible product,

A Company Built on Citric Acid

In 1849, two young German immigrants, Charles Pfizer, 25, and his cousin Charles Erhart, 28, started a modest fine-chemicals business in Brooklyn, New York. It was destined to grow into the modern giant that bears the Pfizer name.

With $2,500 borrowed from Pfizer's father and a $1,000 mortgage, they bought a small building in the Williamsburg section, which was largely German. (So were most of Pfizer's employees; later, when the Brooklyn Navy Yard and Pfizer were the two largest industries on Flushing Avenue, Pfizer was known as the "German Navy Yard.") In those days, the streets were lit by whale-oil lamps, people traveled by stagecoach and

heads of *Artemisia cina* and used to combat parasitic worms. To make it palatable, it was shaped in a candy cone with the bitter medicine disguised by a sugar-cream confection. The partners delivered it on foot in wicker baskets and later by horse and wagon — but only if the roads were not too slippery. When they were, customers had to pick up their orders themselves.

By 1860, the Pfizer line had expanded to include iodine preparations, mercurials, borax, boric acid and camphor. The partners opened an office in downtown Manhattan on Beekman Street, later moving to Maiden Lane. Soon they were importing argols — the encrustation residue left in casks from

leaving Pfizer scrambling for supplies. This set the company off on a long search for a method to produce citric acid from sugar by fermentation alone.

By 1923, the company at last had a practical process based on the common bread mold *Aspergillus niger*. It decided not to patent the process, but to swear everyone who knew the production method to secrecy instead. A seven-story structure was built expressly to make the new product — it was dubbed the SUCIAC building ("Sugar Under Conversion Into Acid Citric"). To meet a seemingly endless demand, it operated around the clock, 365 days a year. In 1934, a major breakthrough came when Pfizer

Charles Pfizer (1824-1906), left, and his cousin Charles Erhart (1821-1891), right, came from Germany to start a small fine-chemicals business in Brooklyn in 1849, when Pfizer was all of 25 years old and Erhart was 28. A painting of their original plant appears on the opposite page.

developed a method of using molasses instead of the much more expensive white sugar, saving millions of dollars in raw material and production costs.

The know-how accumulated in the production of citric acid was to prove invaluable in the later development of fermentation processes for vitamins C and B-12, as well

as antibiotics like streptomycin, penicillin and Terramycin. As late as 1941, citric acid still constituted 46 percent of Pfizer's sales, but as the company emerged as a major force in synthetic drugs, the proportion waned. The citric acid business, the foundation of Pfizer's success, was finally sold in 1990.

In 1946, Pfizer purchased from the U.S. government a surplus World War II submarine shipyard along the banks of the Thames River in Groton, Connecticut. Over many years of growth and rebuilding, the facility has grown into the company's primary research and manufacturing site.

its new product Terramycin because it had been found in the earth, or *terra* in Latin. Its first clinical test was performed, with dramatically successful results, on a pneumonia patient at Harlem Hospital on New Year's Eve.

The product was approved by the U.S. Food and Drug Administration less than three months later, on March 22, 1950, and went on the market that very same month. Pfizer Research had produced its first successful product. At the time, the company had $60 million in annual sales and 3,351 employees.

Still smarting from its penicillin experience, this time Pfizer was not about to market its important new product through other drug companies. Before he died of cancer, Pfizer President John L. Smith told his successor John E. McKeen: "Let's sell it ourselves." And, after much debate, that is just what Pfizer did — to the chagrin of regular Pfizer customers, at least one of whom declared bitterly that henceforth he would buy bulk materials from anyone *but* Pfizer. Two years after its introduction, sales of Terramycin reached an unheard-of $45 million a year, 42 percent of the company's revenues. Within a short time, Pfizer's new manufacturing site at Groton, Connecticut – a former World War II submarine shipyard purchased from the U.S. government in 1946 – would boast the largest fermentation plant in the world. The company increased its sales force from 25 employees in 1949 to 1,300 in 1953. Pfizer had become a full-fledged, research-based drug company specializing in antibiotics derived from fermentation.

It is risky in any business, however, to depend on a single product – doubly so in the pharmaceutical industry, where a discovery like Terramycin stimulates research in the field by competitors, who could now analyze Terramycin and try to develop a drug of their own with improved properties. Wrote Samuel Mines in his 1978 book, *Pfizer...an Informal History*: "Every drug company, therefore, is faced with the problem of recouping its investment and showing some kind of profit before its brainchild begins to feel the hot breath of competition on its neck. Like the Red Queen in *Alice in Wonderland*, it is necessary to run twice as fast merely to stay in the same spot."

In the late 1940s, Pfizer was ill-equipped to run at all, let alone twice as fast. It still had a tiny research staff, consisting mainly of fermentation biologists and engineers, with just one doctoral-level pharmacologist and a handful of organic chemists, all located at the Brooklyn manufacturing plant. In 1948, management had decided to bolster its research leadership with a new director, Wilbur Lazier, who had worked at DuPont and brought to Pfizer much-needed experience in industrial research. Lazier's No. 2 man, Karl Brunings, was, among other things, an outstanding talent scout.

Lazier and Brunings strengthened the company's research capability by bringing in increasing numbers of newly trained organic chemists with doctoral degrees. The 1950 crop alone included Gerald D. Laubach from MIT, William McLamore from Harvard, Robert Feeney from Yale and Lloyd Conover and Rex Pinson from the University of Rochester – each destined to contribute crucially to the company's growth and success.

Competition in the pharmaceutical industry was intense, and the new team clearly had its work cut out. Terramycin was the chemical compound oxytetracycline. Aureomycin, a competing product discovered by American Cyanamid's Lederle Laboratories in 1948, was chlortetracycline. In 1950 the molecular structures of these complex molecules had finally been elucidated by the Pfizer Research team, working with R. B. Woodward of Harvard (later to become a Nobel laureate).

One member of the team, Lloyd Conover, speculated that the side chains of the base molecule could be chemically modified in the lab to increase chemical stability. His colleagues in the industry had not attempted modification of an antibiotic, since prior to Pfizer's invention of tetracycline, scientists had considered it impossible to chemically alter a fermentation-derived, ("natural") antibiotic without the destruction or drastic impairment of its therapeutic activity. Conover was breaking new ground, and his theory was greeted with skepticism. Even if the chemical modification proved successful, there were doubts that the resulting product would be active as an antibiotic.

In June 1952, Conover confounded his colleagues by preparing tetracycline – and showing it to be a powerful antibiotic. He accomplished this by stripping the chlorine atom from the chlortetracycline molecule

Lloyd Conover, above, was the inventor of tetracycline, the first semisynthetic antibiotic, which opened up a new world of drugs for the pharmaceutical industry. In the photo below, the new drug is the topic of conversation among, from left, James Korst, Lloyd Conover, David Johnston and Kenneth Butler.

by hydrogenating chlortetracycline under carefully controlled conditions. This breakthrough process produced a more stable drug and opened up a new world of potential drugs for the pharmaceutical industry. Pfizer's innovative technique initiated the era of semisynthetic antibiotics.

Tetracycline went on to become the most widely prescribed broad-spectrum antibiotic in the United States in the 1950s. Forty years later, in 1992, Lloyd Conover, who had retired in 1983 as Pfizer's senior vice president of Central Research for Agriculture Products R&D, was inducted into the National Inventors Hall of Fame for his discovery. It was an honor that had been extended to only 98 inventors at the time, including Thomas Edison, Eli Whitney, the Wright brothers and Alexander Graham Bell.

Meanwhile, Bill McLamore made his first discovery, a sedative-hypnotic called ethchlorvynol, an acetylenic carbinol related to other compounds used as intermediates in the production of vitamin A, one of Pfizer's major products at the time. Ethchlorvynol was sold by Pfizer in the United Kingdom under the brand name Arvinol. In the United States it was licensed to Abbott, which sold it under the name of Placidyl.

The learning process regarding the connection between fermentation chemistry and new drug compounds continued under a steroid research team headed by Gerald Laubach, which was joined in 1952 by Barry Bloom. Pfizer knew that the mycelia – the vegetative parts of fungi consisting of masses of threadlike tubes – used in the production of citric acid were an abundant source of ergosterol, a crystalline steroid alcohol. It was decided to try to synthesize cortisone – a corticosteroid that had just been reported as a wonder drug – by chemical transformation of ergosterol. Laubach had a brilliant plan that ultimately succeeded, but it failed to produce cortisone economically. In the meantime, Upjohn came up with a more practical manufacturing process, one based on a key fermentation step (known technically as the 11-alpha-hydroxylation of Reichstein's Substance S).

"Pfizer had been beaten at its own game," recalls Barry Bloom. "For several years after that, we did research on microbiological transformations of steroids, had a lot of fun, published well-received findings but didn't make a nickel for Pfizer. A little later on, we collaborated with Syntex on steroid research. Indeed, at one point, Pfizer had an option to acquire the original oral contraceptive, which was discovered at Syntex in 1951. But our corporate management, influenced by religious beliefs, felt that Pfizer should not enter that field."

In the meantime, worldwide demand for Terramycin encouraged the company to start setting up shop abroad, where potential markets were attractive. New offices were opened in 1951 in Puerto Rico, Panama, Mexico and Brazil, followed by Cuba, Canada, the United Kingdom, Belgium, Japan, Spain, Colombia, Venezuela and the Netherlands. It was a risky but momentous step for Pfizer, giving the company an early international presence that few American pharmaceutical companies could match.

The newly created international business went "big time" almost overnight. Nowhere was this truer than in the United Kingdom. At one time during the 1950s, Pfizer had the largest annual revenues of any drug company in Great Britain. That remarkable achievement occurred before Parliament broke the Pfizer market exclusivity on Terramycin by legalizing the importation of oxytetracycline from Italy. But the revenues earned in Great Britain led, nevertheless, to the establishment of Pfizer's pharmaceutical research at Sandwich, England.

Pfizer's U.K. operations had begun in 1952 in Folkestone, but by 1954, production requirements had outgrown the site, and the company found a more suitable site up the coast at Sandwich, a World War I port facility from which troops and matériel had been shipped to France. Despite questions about its structural integrity, one building on this site, the former headquarters for Lord Horatio Kitchener's expeditionary forces, served for many years as the pharmacology building for Pfizer.

Pharmaceutical research started at Sandwich in 1957 with a total of six people – five chemists and one pharmacologist. By the following year, Dick Fenton, an Englishman who was then head of Pfizer's European operations, decided that a whole new research group should be created – a logical move for a multinational pharmaceutical company, which needed discovery research and technical support as part of fully integrated operations overseas. However, the early years of research in Sandwich were handicapped by lack of focus and the absence of effective leadership.

"Some horrendous mistakes were made," recalls Barry Bloom. "They hired a lot of people very quickly,

without much thought. A sizable organization was assembled too fast, virtually overnight. They had no real grasp of how one should organize to carry out research effectively. Specialists were brought in to work in their favorite fields however they saw fit.

"They took on research in virology, about 15 years before the science was ready for that sort of thing. They took on a program in tropical medicine, which has long been dear to the hearts of British scientists. That's all well and good, but once you've discovered a drug, there isn't much you can do with it because in most tropical countries the infrastructure isn't there to supply it to the people who need it most. The net result was that for 15 years the place floundered. It not only didn't accomplish anything; it didn't have a sense of how to go about the business it was supposed to."

Ian Wrigley, who joined Sandwich in 1957 as a chemist and retired as research director in 1986, remembers the awkward problem: "The new organization was the brainchild of Dick Fenton and Pfizer Ltd (the company's new British subsidiary) and he started it pretty much on his own. The people in Groton didn't think very much of Sandwich at all."

Fenton went to an old friend of his, Solly Zuckerman, a professor at Oxford who became chief scientific advisor to the British government. Zuckerman advised Fenton how to go about setting up the organization, what topics to research and, most important of all, to choose a man named Ronald Boscott, who had been a research student of his, to head the operation. "That was Disaster No. 1 because Boscott wasn't the right man," says Wrigley. "He survived for three or four years, but during that period, the research operation at Sandwich could be best described as 'shambolical.'"

No one who worked at Sandwich in the early days will forget a man named Harald Reinert, an extremely capable German pharmacologist but a very arrogant type – "a big liver, a big spender, a big voice, who had no hesitation about speaking his mind," one colleague recalls. Before he came to Pfizer, Reinert had applied for a job at ICI Pharmaceuticals, a major British drug maker, at a time when memories of World War II were still fresh in people's minds. When he arrived at ICI for an interview, he was asked to sign the visitors' book. He entered his name, "H. Reinert," and under the heading "previous affiliation" he wrote "Sixth Panzer Division, Afrika Corps." He didn't get the job.

Reinert did get a job at Pfizer Ltd, however, where he soon imposed his idea that biology and pharmacology should dominate the show. He ran rings around Boscott and thus was effectively in control of Research. There was no coordination of research topics

with Groton. Moreover, there was a crisis of confidence in Sandwich's ability to discover important drugs. Morale was low. A lot of people thought that Sandwich might even be closed down.

Things were not going well on the other side of the Atlantic either. The U.S. research group was split by a schism between the microbiologists, or fermentation people, who had put Pfizer on the map in the 1940s, and the organic chemists, who were making their presence felt during the 1950s. Part of the reason for the split was the fundamental difference in their training and approach to chemistry. Organic chemists design and synthesize new chemicals in their laboratories. Fermentation scientists rely on microorganisms to produce new chemicals which the chemists then isolate. The organic chemists represented a more modern approach, but the fermentation people still ran the show. The frustration level of the organic chemists led to Wilbur Lazier's departure in 1953 after only five years. Factionalism between scientific schools was common in the industry; however, Pfizer was suffering from more than a normal amount of factionalism – microbiologists vs. chemists, Sandwich vs. Groton. These differences took their toll on productivity.

In 1960, to help consolidate its U.S. research operations, the company moved into modern laboratories in

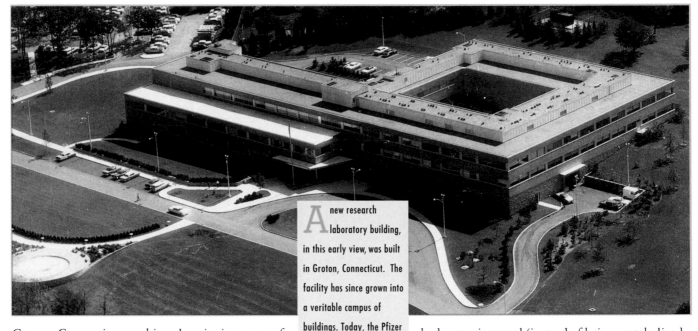

A new research laboratory building, in this early view, was built in Groton, Connecticut. The facility has since grown into a veritable campus of buildings. Today, the Pfizer Central Research Groton campus encompasses 137 acres, 1.5 million square feet of research space and 2,500 employees at this location alone.

Groton, Connecticut, making that site its center of medicinal research. In spite of this impressive new facility, nothing much happened in Groton; the late 1950s and early 1960s were a period of uncertainty and stagnation. The research group seemed to be marking time. Pfizer's pipeline seemed to have dried up with the exception of one star candidate, the antidiabetic medication Diabinese, (chlorpropamide), which McLamore synthesized in a group headed by Laubach. It was the first major medication created by Pfizer Research that was not an antibiotic or a fermentation product. It was also Pfizer's first once-a-day drug due to the drug's tendency to be excreted slowly from the

body once ingested (instead of being metabolized quickly). It not only achieved high sales levels, but it also taught the company the importance of studying drug metabolism, a lesson that was not lost. When it was launched in 1958, Pfizer boasted that Diabinese had cost an incredible $1 million to develop. It was for many years the leading therapy in its field. At the time of Diabinese's launch, Pfizer had $223 million in annual sales.

While Pfizer's research operations groped for a focus, a new problem arose from the political realm. A publicity-seeking Democrat from Tennessee, hoping to further his chances at a presidential nomination, launched an all-

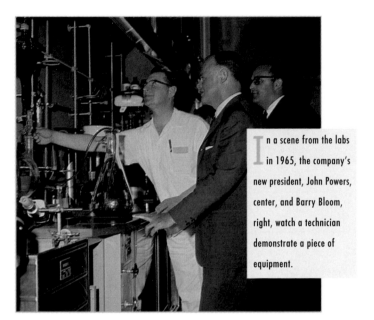

In a scene from the labs in 1965, the company's new president, John Powers, center, and Barry Bloom, right, watch a technician demonstrate a piece of equipment.

out attack on the prescription drug industry in 1959. Senator Estes Kefauver – the man in the famous coonskin cap – had made a reputation investigating organized crime in America. He used as his venue the Senate Subcommittee on Antitrust and Monopoly, of which he was chairman.

Kefauver zeroed in on drug prices, charging that the markup on drugs was 1,000 percent – as high as 7,000 percent in some cases. (The figures were reached by comparing the cost of raw materials with the finished selling price – conveniently ignoring the costs of research, production, distribution and sales.) He lambasted the industry's promotional practices and questioned product safety, with Diabinese as one of his

targets. He was brilliant at manipulating the media. (He was later quoted as saying, "You've got to have an issue, and then you've got to stir up the people.")

Nevertheless, it is doubtful that new legislation would have been passed had it not been for the thalidomide tragedy, in which it was discovered that a drug taken as a sedative by pregnant mothers between 1959 and 1962 resulted in as many as 3,000 horribly deformed babies in West Germany and 500 in Great Britain. The drug had not been distributed for use in the United States because of delays in regulatory approval not related to birth defects. (Thalidomide's potential for harm had not been detected in the safety tests used then. Preclinical tests capable of showing effects on the fetus are done today.)

Fears aroused by thalidomide gave Kefauver his issue, and in 1962 Congress passed the Kefauver-Harris Amendments to the Food, Drug and Cosmetic Act, which extended governmental control beyond finished pharmaceutical products to the very process of creating them. Paradoxically, the new law imposed severe regulations not on drug safety tests but on effectiveness-testing procedures, turning new drug development into a considerably more costly and time-consuming process. The regulatory burden raised the cost of drug research and development, forced many smaller pharmaceutical

Key scientists pose behind some of the volumes of data on Pfizer drug candidates submitted to the FDA in the 1960s. From left: S. Y. P'an, Safety Evaluation; R. L. Wagner, Analytical Research; C. E. Askelson, Agricultural R&D; Sheldon Gilgore, Clinical Research; R. Keith Blackwood, Process Research; R. B. Stebbins, Pathology; and F. A. Hochstein, Chemical Services.

companies out of business, caused others to hedge their bets by diversifying into other fields and led to a "drug lag" between the United States and other countries where regulations were less onerous and new drugs could reach the market faster.

Says Barry Bloom: "Little did we know then how profound the impact would ultimately be of FDA entry into the world of drug research. From the very first moment that you propose to take an experimental drug into clinical trials the government is your overseer, your part-

ner, your auditor and your boss. The terribly intrusive oversight of clinical research by the FDA bureaucracy (which has grown to almost 10,000 people) has created an environment in which little room is left for imaginative thinking and serendipitous observation — it far exceeds anything that is necessary, and is probably the most negative influence on therapeutic innovation that exists today."

"It was all very simple back in the Terramycin days," says Rex Pinson, retired vice president, Medicinal

Products R&D. "George Stone, director of Commercial Development, would put a quarter- to a half-inch-thick document in his briefcase, which said the product was safe in rats, and go to Washington with it. There were also testimonials from a number of doctors who said they'd used it and that it worked. Then, if the FDA hadn't objected within six months, you could sell the drug. After Kefauver, the requirements that, in addition to safety, efficacy be demonstrated became part of the picture. Nobody objected to this in principle. However, they did object to it when, in a New Drug Application, more and more evidence of efficacy would be required long after efficacy was no longer in doubt."

Under new burdens imposed by the FDA, the early 1960s continued to be difficult years for Pfizer Research. Little emerged from the company's discovery efforts. Feeling the pressure of stringent FDA regulation, Pfizer management began to acquire other, non-pharmaceutical businesses as a way of hedging against the future – including the Barbasol Company, makers of shaving creams and toiletries; the Desitin Chemical Company, manufacturers of dermatological and baby-care products; and Coty, Inc., maker of a world-famous line of perfumes and cosmetics. At one point, the company even considered buying the Taylor Wine Company in the Finger Lakes

district of upper New York State. ("Thank goodness we didn't," says Bloom. "We probably would have tried to make wine by deep-tank fermentation, using molasses instead of grapes!")

Then, in 1963, came a turning point. Chairman of the Board John McKeen had asked Vice Chairman Jack Powers to shake up the Research Division and get it

John E. McKeen, president from 1949 to 1965, knew thousands of employees by name. He was known for putting an arm around a fellow Pfizer employee's shoulder and asking, "What's new?"

moving again. Within six months Powers had made Gerald Laubach director of U.S. Medicinal Products Research – an organic chemist was replacing Ernest Weber, a fermentation man. Laubach moved quickly to create a modern research management system, introducing multidisciplinary discovery project teams and annual strategic operating plans. Powers himself provided a series of questions for Pfizer scientists to answer – What kind of drug are you seeking? Why? What leads have you got? What methods of assay are you using? These questions and answers were captured in a document which became known as a project abstract, a method still in use today. It was mainly Laubach, however, who provided the new atmosphere for Research.

As he revitalized the Research Division, the new product famine gave way to a veritable feast. During the late 1960s and early 1970s, Pfizer had more new drugs approved by the FDA than any other pharmaceutical company, despite a modest research budget that by 1972 still had not reached $25 million. Important products developed in this period in Pfizer's Groton research labs included Renese, a diuretic (1962); Vibramycin, a key antibiotic (1967); Navane, an antipsychotic (1967); and Sinequan, to treat depression (1969).

Vibramycin, or doxycycline, emerged from a research program to modify existing tetracyclines which was headed by Charles Stephens and included Keith Blackwood, John Beereboom and Hans Rennhard. Manfred Schach von Wittenau came to the group around 1960.

Out of this program had also come a compound named Rondomycin; it met exactly the specifications of the Marketing Division, which wanted a drug better than Lederle's Declomycin, a big commercial success. With Rondomycin, Pfizer headquarters felt that the potential of the tetracyclines had been reached, although Rondomycin turned out to be a bust on the market, since it was too similar to competitive agents. Al Greene, then the corporate officer responsible for Research, believing doxycycline to be too costly to produce and not worth pursuing, forbade further work to determine either the superior therapeutic effects or the dosage range for the new compound.

"I happened at that time to have doxycycline in the test tube and had done some work with pharmacokinetics testing in animals," recalls Schach von Wittenau. "I had convinced myself that it was a better compound than Rondomycin, and I kept on working at it when I wasn't supposed to.

"I had developed a pretty good case at about the time that Jack Powers put Gerry Laubach in charge of Research. I was able to convince Rex Pinson, and with him Laubach, that doxycycline was a viable drug, and he seized the opportunity to develop it. I don't think it ever would have seen the light of day had I not acted against orders and kept working on the compound." Jim Korst later carried out the important lab research that provided a commercially viable production process.

Vibramycin, the first once-a-day, broad-spectrum antibiotic, was a big success for Pfizer, but not before it became the focus of a major lawsuit in 1973. A company named International Rectifier, which had had a long history of challenging patents in the tetracycline area, signed a contract with U.S. Vitamin, a Revlon subsidiary, to manufacture Vibramycin, having picked up the formula from the published literature. International Rectifier attempted to argue that Pfizer's patent was invalid and unenforceable, one of the arguments being that the patent was procured by inequitable conduct before the U.S. Patent Office. The suit dragged on for many years, but Pfizer eventually won, and Rectifier was enjoined to leave the market.

Vibramycin proved a boon to the company for many years. It required only 10 percent of the dose prescribed for Terramycin and was notable for its speed of absorption, its long-lasting blood levels and the absence of gastric upset as a side effect. Its enduring medical value can be measured by its wide use even today, more than 25 years later, to cure infections around the world.

Close on the heels of Vibramycin came Geopen, a semi-synthetic penicillin; Mithracin, an antitumor antibiotic; Lithane, for the treatment of manic depressive syndrome; Geocillin, an oral form of Geopen; Fasigyn, an antiprotozoral used especially for vaginal infection; and Mecadox, an antibacterial for swine.

With products such as these, and a new spirit humming, the stage was set for the next chapter in the Pfizer story, under the aegis of Central Research. Laubach had done so well revamping Research that in 1968 he was called to New York headquarters to help overhaul Pfizer Pharmaceuticals as its boss, marking the end of his career as a practicing scientist. In 1971, as executive vice president of the company, he supervised the integration of all of Pfizer's worldwide research arms into a newly created Central Research Division – a move that would have profound significance in the years to come.

it was obvious that it was going to be a great company, and we were all part of it."

Gerry Laubach and his colleagues Rex Pinson, now retired vice president for Medicinal Products, and medicinal chemist Eugene Agnello tried to synthesize cortisone using materials extracted from the waste products of citric acid fermentation. Barry Bloom, a graduate of the same MIT research program as Laubach, joined Pfizer and the cortisone project in 1952. Although the

ology offered a new understanding of how drugs work at the molecular level. As the paper showed, drug discovery would, in the future, rely less on chance and more on knowledge.

Laubach was a pioneer in recognizing the importance of mission-oriented research and the benefit of multidisciplinary project teams whereby chemists, biologists, toxicologists, clinical investigators and other R&D specialists pooled their knowledge, rather

Gerald D. Laubach

The year 1950, which saw the launch of Terramycin, was also the starting date at Pfizer of Gerald D. Laubach, a 24-year-old organic chemist with a Ph.D. from the Massachusetts Institute of Technology.

It was the Golden Age of antibiotics, and Gerald D. Laubach was just one among a number of young chemists and biologists attracted to Pfizer's fledgling research group. The size of the group and the facilities they had to work with remained modest through the ensuing decade, but their energy and enthusiasm seemed unlimited.

Recalls Robert Feeney, retired vice president of Licensing and Development: "They were wonderful times. Pfizer was small, but

group eventually did synthesize cortisone, the process was never considered practical enough to be applied commercially.

Until this time, research at Pfizer was empirical – trial and error – and relied heavily on fermentation. Under the leadership of research directors Wilbur Lazier and Karl Brunings, a more systematic approach was adopted, stressing planning, record-keeping, communication and the application of pure science to industrial research. In 1962, Laubach and Bloom co-authored a scientific paper that showed the relationship between the structure of chemical compounds and their pharmaceutical activity and pointed out that growing knowledge about human physi-

than working in isolation, as they had been until then. A novel concept at the time, the project teams markedly increased the efficiency of R&D.

Laubach, who had joined Pfizer's board of directors in 1968, was among the first in the industry to raise awareness of the "drug lag," the effect of regulatory delay in getting new drugs to patients who needed them. In 1971, as the company's executive vice president, Laubach supervised the integration of all of Pfizer's research organizations into a new Central Research Division, headquartered in Groton, Connecticut. At the end of 1972, when Jack Powers announced his retirement, Edmund T. Pratt, Jr., became chairman and

CEO and Laubach became president, a post he filled with distinction for 18 years until his retirement in 1991. As a tribute, the company renamed a department chair it had endowed for several years at MIT (Laubach's old alma mater) in his honor.

In the 1970s and 1980s, Laubach took a strong leadership role in efforts to reform the drug regulatory process, as well as in a broad range of connected policy issues of importance to Pfizer and the health-care industry. Among them were health-care cost containment, the role of science and technological innovation in our society, math and science education and intellectual property protection. He served on President Reagan's Commission on Industrial Competitiveness, on the National Association of Manufacturers' Committee on Innovation, Technology and Science Policy and as chairman of the Pharmaceutical Manufacturers Association. A leading health publication described Laubach as a "quiet but formidable figure within the industry." Says William C. Steere, Jr., his successor as Pfizer's president: "Gerry was like the dean of health policy in the country; people came to him for his opinions and views. As a result, Pfizer has played a leading role in shaping health policy."

As a leading advocate for innovation in health care, Laubach once said: "The princi-

Gerald Laubach supervised the formation of a new Central Research Division in 1971, then served as president of the company for 18 years.

pal reason for the rapid acceptance of novel [pharmaceutical] technology is that the drug is frequently an effective alternative to surgery. A significant modern pharmaceutical can quickly change the prevalent mode of health care, and sometimes substantially reduce its cost. Pfizer policy is to discover and develop new drug products that are so innovative it would be unconscionable to deny their use."

3

The Beginning of Worldwide Central Research

A chemist in Pfizer's Cancer Research Department in Groton, examines a compound. With the creation of Central Research in 1971, departments such as Cancer Research stretched beyond national boundaries as research teams accessed the talents of scientists all over the globe, with coordination of the research by a centralized management.

Pfizer had successfully relocated its research facilities, but the organization and management of its research and development efforts remained fragmented. In 1971, the leadership at Pfizer Inc decided to bring all of the research and development activities conducted for new pharmaceuticals, fine chemicals, and animal health under the umbrella of a new worldwide division to be called Central Research. The formal announcement was issued on September 23, 1971.

Barry Bloom was appointed Central Research's first president. "I was deeply impressed with Bloom," recalls Powers. "He was ideal – the scientist, the intellectual, but also a very human person. Running a big research organization, you've got to have that human touch and not just be an intellectual in an ivory tower. One of the reasons I decided to go worldwide with the research effort was Barry Bloom himself – he's just an extraordinary person."

Gerry Laubach supported management's commitment to reorganize Pfizer's research efforts into a Central Research Division, but he felt that Pfizer should be hedging its position by broadening out into other businesses, such as hospital products, rather than greatly increasing its investment in research and development. His principal motivation was concern about the massive growth of regulatory oversight of the pharmaceutical industry, which even then was becoming oppressive in the United States. This trend in regulatory growth did not bode well for the pharmaceutical innovator, he felt.

Laubach – characterized as a "gloomy visionary" by some of his peers – had a great deal of insight about the future but tended to be relatively pessimistic about it. He could see difficulties emerging for the pharmaceutical business – strong pressures on pricing and on freedom of choice – many of which eventually came to pass as he predicted.

As a result, in the early 1970s, Pfizer Inc was again looking to diversify outside of pharmaceuticals. Some investments were related to health care, such as the major purchase of Howmedica in 1972, a company producing orthopedic, dental and prosthetic devices. Acquisition of Holgrath (needles, syringes), DeKnatel

(sutures), United Surgical (wound dressings, plaster casts), Valley Labs (electrosurgical equipment), Shiley (heart valves) and Myerson Tooth (dental cement) broadened the product line for the Pfizer division that came to be known as the Hospital Products Group (HPG). Other ventures for Pfizer included joint production of the CAT Scanner and Autobac machines for diagnosis of diseases, as well as ventures with, and acquisition of, companies that produced such items as high-quality magnetic oxides for recording tapes, new types of seed corn, cosmetics (Coty) and linings for steel furnaces. Pfizer was indeed moving away from pharmaceuticals.

Though the atmosphere among Pfizer management regarding the potential of Central Research was tentative – for example, its formation received less than a sentence of explanation in the 1972 annual report – Barry Bloom, head of Central Research, never felt that his job was in jeopardy. Instead, backed by Gerald Laubach, he convinced management that research timelines were by nature long and that "quick fixes" to finding new pharmaceuticals were not possible. As a result, there was a feeling of confidence within Central Research that the corporation would be supportive over the years of research needed to find new drugs.

The centerpiece of the new division Bloom was to organize was headquartered in Groton, Connecticut, and would include laboratories in Sandwich, Kent, in the U.K.; Amboise, France; Terre Haute, Indiana; and Nagoya, Japan. What Bloom encountered when he began the reorganization, however, was a factionalized research effort that lacked the focus and collaboration necessary to efficiently discover and develop viable new drug products. Bloom set out to build an integrated, worldwide R&D force.

Groton, Connecticut

Prior to 1960, Pfizer's research in the U.S. was scattered among several sites – including synthetic chemistry and analytical and formulation laboratories in Brooklyn and pharmacology laboratories in Maywood, New Jersey. This geographical spread hindered the close communications and interactions that are critical to a team effort in a complex scientific project. As Pfizer's research expenditures grew from about $10 million to about $200 million over the decade of the 1950s, the number of people in research grew from a total of less than 500 to more than 750. Lab space in the Brooklyn laboratories was filled to capacity, and further growth required a new site.

John J. Powers, Jr., president of Pfizer from 1965 to 1971, looks on while his predecessor John E. McKeen examines a slide through a microscope. On the opposite page, a statue of Hermes, messenger of the gods who mythically brought medicine to man, adorns the main entrance to the buildings of Central Research in Groton.

Since proximity of *all* the major scientific disciplines was seen as a valued objective, a search was undertaken for a new site, one large enough for an integrated research facility and with enough space for future expansion.

After considering possible sites in New Jersey and elsewhere, senior management settled on Groton, Connecticut, where the company already had a manufacturing facility and owned some adjacent property. The Groton research facility opened in late 1959 and was dedicated on October 6, 1960 at a gala ceremony attended by over a thousand guests, including the governor of Connecticut, Governor Abraham Ribicoff. This new 177,000-square-foot facility – on 19 acres, with a modern technical library containing 18,000 volumes – brought together the chemists, biologists, toxicologists, clinicians, developmental research scientists and all the other team members who are necessary for a successful R&D organization. A 28-foot mosaic at the main entrance symbolized the dawn of new knowledge and the emergence of laboratory research. A 20-foot bronze sculpture of Hermes on a granite pedestal was placed at the front of the new facility to remind all who worked here of this messenger of the gods who brought gifts of medicine and pharmacy to earth.

Sandwich, U.K.

Pfizer Ltd, the company's international British subsidiary, had been in existence at Sandwich for nearly 20 years, and by 1971, Pfizer Research was operating in Sandwich with a staff of 406 and a budget of $5 million. Some accomplishments of the Sandwich Research Group in the 1960s and 1970s were the discovery and development of the schistosomicidal agent, oxaminiquine, and the beta-blocker, tolamolol. The discovery of oxaminiquine in 1968 took advantage of insightful chemical manipulations to make a conformationally restricted analog of a precursor compound. Successful clinical trials were carried out in Brazil and Africa, showing that oxaminiquine was effective as single oral doses, unlike previous treatments which required multiple doses of i.v. drugs.

Above, Pfizer Chairman John Powers, flanked by Bill Roche and Brian Carmichael, visits the Sandwich facility in 1969. Today, Pfizer Ltd at Sandwich employs nearly 3,000 people, half of them in manufacturing, half in research. The West Site Research Campus, below, is across the road from the plant and linked to it by a pedestrian bridge. The relatively new, attractively landscaped buildings are leading examples of modern architectural design.

Launched in 1975 as Mansil, the drug was very well tolerated and was added to the *Who's Who* list of essential drugs in 1977.

Tolamolol's discovery arose out of a program to find a cardioselective beta-blocker. Discovered in 1969, tolamolol proved much more cardioselective than marketed drugs and was much better tolerated. After several years of clinical research, a finding of mammary tumors in rats caused withdrawal of tolamolol from development.

Ian Wrigley, a young chemist at the time, remembers well the day in 1971 that CEO Jack Powers came to Sandwich on a fact-finding mission, despite a leg in a cast from a torn Achilles tendon: "He really grilled everybody about research. He met every single person in the Research Division, down to the junior lab technicians. Since he couldn't get around very well, there was a constant parade of people going in to see him."

It was only a few weeks after his visit that Powers put out a memo creating the new Central Research Division under Corporate Executive Vice President Gerald Laubach with Bloom as divisional president. With centralized coordination of all Pfizer's research activities, the separate ways of life at Sandwich and Groton were about to change.

As one of his first moves, Bloom named Lloyd Conover as Sandwich's new Research director, replacing James Morrison. "I remember it very clearly," Conover recalls. "I was standing in the lunch line in the Groton cafeteria and Barry came over and said, 'I'd like to see you in my office after you finish your lunch.' I thought, 'Ye gods, what have I done now?' When I got there, he said, 'I'd like you to work in Sandwich for three years, taking over as Research director from Jimmy Morrison.'

"I said, 'How about one year?'

"Anyway, he gave me until December to make a final decision. Ginny, my wife, had been agitating for a trip to England but was decidedly unenthusiastic about living there for three years. My youngest son, who was 15 and a high school sophomore, said simply, 'I'm not going.' (He finally did go.)

Pictured below are three of the men who brought Pfizer to greatness. From left: Gerald D. Laubach, president from 1972 to 1991; Edmund T. Pratt, Jr., chairman from 1972 to 1992; and John J. Powers, Jr., chairman from 1968 to 1972.

"I don't remember the words used by Barry to describe my mission, but I'm sure the message went something like this: 'Sandwich has not been productive; report-writing is terrible; morale is poor; the budgets are chronically overspent; they have too many discovery projects for the number of scientists; there are too many speculative discovery approaches. Whip Sandwich into shape."

When Conover arrived, he found that morale indeed was terrible. ("It seemed to me that Sandwich had been a classical case of mushroom management – keep 'em in the dark and feed 'em manure.") People down in the labs thought that decisions were being made by managers who did not understand what was going on and who did not consult those who did. There was great sensitivity because Sandwich Research had not produced a commercially successful new drug for human use. Lab scientists felt they were not being paid enough to make ends meet.

"Sending over an American was not an easy judgment call," Bloom recalls. "The Brits had a lot of pride. But Conover was the right man for the right job at the right time. He'd had a distinguished career as a scientist, he was an experienced manager and he had the kind of personality that would enable him to develop good relationships. And that's exactly the way it worked out."

"The Brits" had long recognized that there was something wrong with the way they were organized and with their approach to doing research in an industrial setting. "There was a lot of science for science's sake," remembers Dion Butt, then a biochemist at Sandwich. "A lot of people were just working on things that interested them. The chemists were doing their thing, the biologists their thing, and there was only loose contact between them. There was a certain lack of focus."

"They badly wanted leadership that could tell them what they ought to be doing," says Bloom. "So there was no lack of willingness to cooperate, and the result was that Sandwich turned the corner, once and for all. Indeed, the old days came to be jokingly referred to as the years B.C. – Before Conover!"

To make a fresh start, Pfizer management moved Harald Reinert to head Pfizer's new drug safety evaluation laboratories in Amboise, France, and dispensed with the services of the head clinician, another controversial

Ian Wrigley served as Pfizer's director of Research at Sandwich, England, from 1975 to 1986, succeeding Lloyd Conover, whom Wrigley credits with turning Sandwich around. During Wrigley's tenure, the site became the largest research operation of any American pharmaceutical company outside the U.S.

type, before Conover's arrival. Others who didn't fit the game plan either left on their own or were given good reason to leave. New people moved up to greater responsibility.

Says Ian Wrigley, "It only took two or three weeks of Lloyd Conover to see that he was out to make the place work. A new structure was created, a new atmosphere. The long-term therapeutic objectives of Sandwich and Groton were defined, and the assignments divvied up. There was also to be greater collaboration on clinical trial work on each other's drugs. The whole ethos of the place changed; it became a serious, proper, professional operation. Though there were at first no major successes in discovering new drugs, morale improved."

In 1973, in an effort to expand clinical research beyond the U.K. and into continental Europe, Bloom introduced the idea of "Euroclin", a nickname (that has stuck) for a new kind of research structure across Europe to conduct the clinical trials required for submission of drugs to regulatory authorities throughout the world. Organized and created by Conover, Euroclin originally consisted of the Sandwich U.K. Clinical Department and a group of four newly hired

medical doctors based in offices at the Pfizer European
Management Center in Brussels. Both the Sandwich
and Brussels units reported to Michael O'Neil-East,
director of Clinical Research. Initially, the new hires
worked on clinical studies in Switzerland, Scandinavia,
Germany, France, Belgium and Holland. Before long
satellite offices were opened in France, Germany and
then one for the Scandinavian countries. After about
two years, Phase I facilities were set up on one floor of a
private clinic called San Remi in Brussels.

Pfizer hired a head-hunting agency to find an
overall director for Euroclin to report to O'Neil East, but
none of the candidates proved suitable. Thus O'Neil-East
himself headed the operation for three years, commuting
from Sandwich to Brussels on a regular basis.

Today Euroclin, which arranges and oversees clinical trials in many countries, employs about 250 people;
it also has branches in Sweden, Norway, Denmark, Fin-
land, Italy, Spain and the Benelux countries, in addition
to the headquarters in Sandwich. It is headed by David
McGibney, who took over in 1991 from John Henderson.
In 1992, an office was opened in Sydney, Australia, giving the company the opportunity to run once-seasonal
clinical trials on drugs year round. New offices have also
opened in India and Israel. Office staff numbers vary
from Brussels, Paris and Munich, each with about 10

A group of managers and scientists poses near an apt street sign at the company's facility in Karlsruhe, Germany, around 1970.

people, to Copenhagen, where there is an office manager, a clinical research associate and a secretary. Most of the staffers are native to their countries, so there are few intercultural problems.

Data from clinical trials, designed and supported by Pfizer and conducted mainly by physicians associated with teaching hospitals throughout Europe and other parts of the world, is routinely assembled and sent to Sandwich. A computer system called PfizerClin was developed by Pfizer to store all clinical data and to facilitate the production of registration documents for regulatory agencies. The information is conveyed on case-report forms completed by the site physician for each patient, collated, entered into computer format, analyzed and turned into study reports. Data collected in one country is as good as data collected in another country since Euroclin operates to the standards of Good Clinical Practice, and to European Community guidelines, which became effective in January 1993. These standards specify precisely how studies should be conducted and what the obligations of the investigator and sponsor are.

Euroclin is unique. "I don't think any other U.S. pharmaceutical research organization has ever attempted to set up clinical offices across the face of Europe," says Barry Bloom. Others have clinical offices, but only as part of their in-country commercial operations.

Nagoya, Japan

The transformation was not limited to Sandwich. Pfizer was also establishing a presence on the other side of the globe. As far back as 1955, Pfizer had been interested in Japan and formed a 50/50 joint venture with the Taito Sugar Company, which produced molasses,

Employees in uniform gather in front of Pfizer's manufacturing plant near Nagoya, Japan. An early research mission here was screening soil samples for new antibiotics.

used as a raw material in fermentation processes for the manufacture of antibiotics. By 1966, Pfizer-Taito had 1,000 employees and was No. 1 in sales among the Pfizer group outside the United States.

To give the company a research presence in Japan, and to take advantage of local skills in fermentation technology, a soil-screening group was established in 1972 at Pfizer-Taito's new manufacturing plant at Taketoyo, about 25 miles from Nagoya, the third-largest metropolitan area in Japan. Its mission was to isolate new microorganisms from soil samples collected in Japan and other parts of the world, to ferment these microorganisms and to screen the broths produced for new antibiotics for potential human use. When the group encountered an "activity hit" that appeared promising, an extract concentrate was prepared and sent to Groton or Sandwich for further study. From 1975 on, animal health targets were added – coccidiostats, anthelmintics and ectoparasiticides. By that time, the operation consisted of 28 persons, heavily weighted toward non-doctoral degree personnel.

The introduction of a product patent law in the mid-1970s marked the advent of modern medicinal discovery in Japan by offering protection for new pharmaceutical products. The Japanese pharmaceutical industry grew in a few short years to international stature and demonstrated uncommon productivity. Pfizer later expanded their Japan operations to include some research laboratories with synthetic chemistry capabilities.

Amboise, France

Central Research operations in Europe grew in complexity and sophistication with the expansion of a research site in Amboise, east of Tours in the Loire Valley of France. The drug evaluation center there, started in 1970 next door to a Pfizer France packaging plant, began with 30 or 40 people doing research to determine

the preclinical safety of compounds destined for the European market. In 1971, the center was expanded to test new drugs for their long-term toxicity and potential adverse effects on reproductive function, a science known as teratology. Rather than refurbish the animal laboratories at Sandwich, it was decided to close down toxicolog-

A researcher at Amboise, France, examines a computer printout of data concerning the latest test results.

ical research there and concentrate on Amboise, where there was room to expand.

Alastair Monro, now director of external scientific affairs for drug safety evaluation in Groton, was sent to Amboise in 1976 to replace Harald Reinert, who retired. Says Monro: "By now the staff was about 100 – veterinarians, pharmacologists, biologists, pathologists – and our main business was preclinical toxicology. This multidisciplinary activity involves the study, as required by

Most of the 130 employees at Amboise are French nationals. Monro was impressed by their loyalty to Pfizer, despite the fact that they were so far away from the action: "They always appreciated visits from Sandwich and Groton people."

Terre Haute, Indiana

Not only did the formation of Central Research help Pfizer maximize the benefits of the global marketplace, it also sharpened up the organization and efficiency of the laboratories at home. Established in 1952, the laboratory at Terre Haute, Indiana, though productive, was considered remote from the happenings in Groton and Sandwich. In 1975, Lloyd Conover, fresh from his triumphs at Sandwich, was asked to organize an Agricultural Products R&D Division. Animal Health R&D had for some years been marking time without centralized management. Chemists, biologists and veterinarians in Groton, Terre Haute and Sandwich were to be part of a single transatlantic group having centralized management of both discovery and development.

Says Bloom: "One of the great strengths of Central Research today is that it is a truly integrated operation; Groton, Sandwich, Amboise and Nagoya operate interdependently, sharing projects. People are in contact with one another constantly with regard to programs and strategies. It's unique. Not many companies have been

Pfizer's Central Research center in Amboise, France, began operations in 1970. Not long after, the facility was expanded to allow the testing of potential new human drugs on animals.

law, of the adverse effects of candidate drugs administered to animals at exaggerated dose levels and an evaluation of the likelihood that such effects will occur in patients. Where possible, alternative in vitro test systems were also used. Investigations included laboratory tests and clinical examination of the function of the major body systems, histopathological examination of a wide range of body organs and tissues and tests of reproductive function and development of the offspring."

successful in integrating their research in Europe, Japan and the United States."

This was the major objective in the creation of Central Research – to make drug research and development more efficient and more successful by providing one set of management to delegate projects, set focused goals for each laboratory and coordinate their collaborations. The formation of Central Research enabled Pfizer to delegate projects to various labs to coordinate their efforts and to build on local expertise by enabling each laboratory to focus on a specialized area. Thus, the diverse laws, regulations and market of each country – which raised difficulties for many pharmaceutical companies in their international ventures – became an asset for Pfizer when Central Research became part of the organization.

The Growth of Central Research: Disappointments and Successes In the 1970s

The decade of the 1970s was a period of trial and adjustment for this new organizational structure. Growth at Central Research was sporadic – and generally modest – in the first 10 years. Part of the reason for the division's slow growth during

At the laboratories in Terre Haute, Indiana, every ounce counts. Here, a technician checks the weight of a little chick.

this time was that some major products failed at the very last phases of development due to toxicity findings. Corporate management realized that these failures, as in any experimentation, were unavoidable; however, without tangible successes, Central Research was destined to remain at a plateau in terms of both funding and research staffing.

Meanwhile, the situation in Sandwich showed steady improvement. At one point, the scientists there were in a close race with SmithKline French to develop the first H2 antagonist to control ulcers. The chemical series they opted for, however, proved a loser on toxicological grounds, and the rest is history – written by SmithKline's Tagamet, which went on to become a huge success.

In 1975, the program in tropical diseases, which had begun 10 years before, finally resulted in the launching of Mansil, a medicine that the World Health Organization subsequently declared to be the drug of choice for the treatment of schistosomiasis, or snail fever, a parasitic worm infection common in tropical areas. It was unique in that it cured the disease after a single dose, with a cure rate of 90 percent.

Mansil was a successful drug in principle, but it highlighted the problems of tropical medicine: not only could few people in poor countries afford it, but there was no medical or distributional infrastructure for getting it to patients. The only reason that Mansil was success-fully applied at all was because the Brazilian government started a program attempting to eradicate schistosomia-sis and chose Mansil as the drug to be used. Mansil sub-sequently won the Queen's Award for Technological Achievement in 1979.

At about the same time, Sandwich made its first discovery of major commercial potential, an antihyper-tensive drug of the beta-blocker family called tolamalol. It seemed destined to become a revolutionary therapy in the cardiovascular area, the next Pfizer blockbuster after Vibramycin. But at the eleventh hour, when the New Drug Application was almost finished, a strange malfunc-tion was discovered in the mammary glands of rats that had been given the highest dose for an extended period.

It appeared that tolamolol had a unique problem: it was too nontoxic. Researchers were unable to attain toxic levels in rats even with doses many thousands of times that of a dose producing pharmacological activity. At such doses other manifestations, such as mammary

tumors, began to appear that had no relation to the mechanism of the drug. ("It's similar to the obscure fact that if you give a man enough water, it will kill him," observed one researcher.) It is now recognized that this

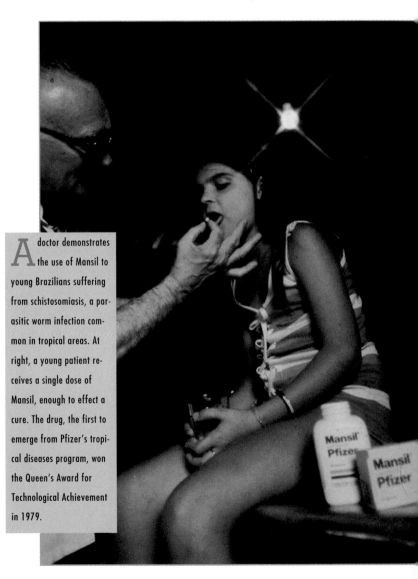

A doctor demonstrates the use of Mansil to young Brazilians suffering from schistosomiasis, a par-asitic worm infection com-mon in tropical areas. At right, a young patient re-ceives a single dose of Mansil, enough to effect a cure. The drug, the first to emerge from Pfizer's tropi-cal diseases program, won the Queen's Award for Technological Achievement in 1979.

particular type of tumor is caused by many other drugs and that it is peculiar to rats. But at that time, anything at all that smacked of drug-induced cancer was the kiss of death. There was no hope of getting the FDA to accept the fact that this was a pharmacological peculiarity and not a toxicological event of significance to man, so Pfizer dropped the whole idea.

"In hindsight, there was no reason for stopping tolamalol," says Dion Butt. "But we couldn't have gotten it approved by the FDA at that time. It was very bad luck, and it was very bad for morale."

"Tolamalol would have been Sandwich's first major product," says Barry Bloom. "It would have been a blockbuster – in its day, it probably would have been the number one cardiovascular drug. It was a heartbreaker for Pfizer."

In the ups and downs of drug discovery during Central Research's first decade, a bright light was the launching of Minipress as a prescription drug in the United States in 1976. It was the brainchild of Hans-Jurgen Hess, former vice president of Medicinal Products Research, now retired, who began working on antihypertensive drugs at Groton as far back as 1963.

At the time, hypertension was one of the world's most under-treated diseases. Many patients stopped taking the existing drugs for lowering blood pressure be-

cause they developed a tolerance to them, or because the drugs altered their metabolism or interfered with the functioning of their hearts, kidneys or intestines. Hess sought a compound that would act selectively, lowering blood pressure by blocking receptors on the smooth muscle cells of blood vessels, causing them to dilate and increase blood flow.

More than a decade later, after testing hundreds of candidates, Hess came up with prazosin which looked as though it would work. Then began the long process toward regulatory approval. When that had been secured, Minipress soon became a leading agent for treatment of high blood pressure. The long years of work paid off in another way: in 1991, Hess received the Pharmaceutical Manufacturers Association's prestigious Drug Discoverer's Award. He was the first Pfizer scientist to achieve that honor, joining 19 previous recipients, three of whom had been Nobel laureates in medicine.

Less fortunate was another promising compound developed at Groton. Tibric acid, invented by Gerald Holland, was a regulator of lipid levels, inducing liver cells to manufacture more of the protein that causes fats to be broken down, metabolized and disposed of by the body, and was thought to be potentially useful in preventing high levels of cholesterol and atherosclerosis. A pathologist who looked at the effect of tibric acid on

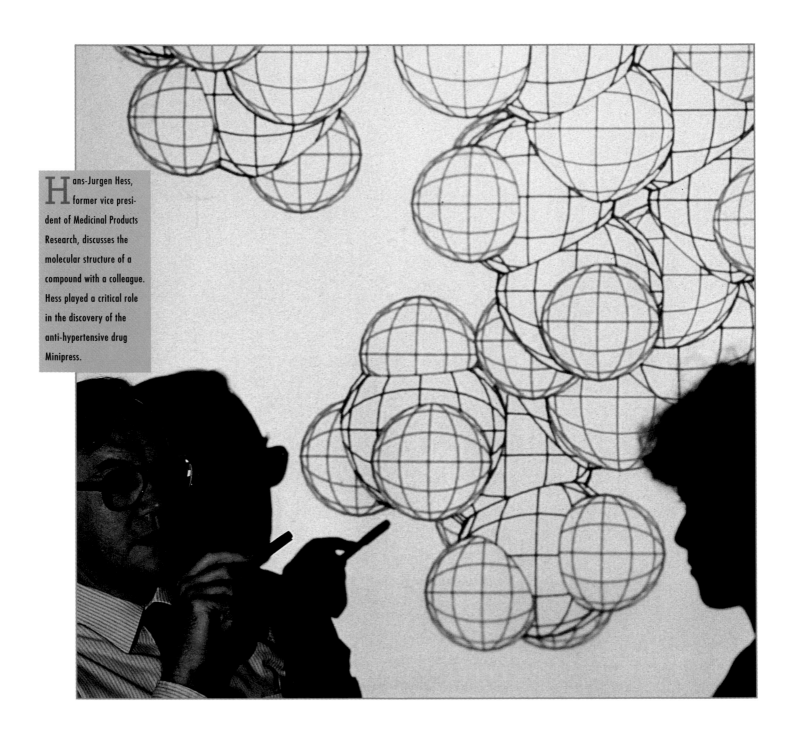

Hans-Jurgen Hess, former vice president of Medicinal Products Research, discusses the molecular structure of a compound with a colleague. Hess played a critical role in the discovery of the anti-hypertensive drug Minipress.

Two of the creators of Feldene, Joseph Lombardino, right, and Edward Wiseman discuss its molecular structure in the laboratory at Groton.

liver cells under a microscope, however, read that as a toxic event because what he saw was an accumulation of a protein above normal levels.

"We had long discussions as to whether this was benign or tumorigenic," recalls Edward H. "Ted" Wiseman, now executive director of Research Administration. "The pathologists won, and it was designated as pretumorigenic. It was really semantics. Indeed, there is a drug on the market that works by exactly the same mechanism; it was developed some years before tibric acid, when the state of the art of pathology was not as

advanced, and the phenomenon probably went undetected. But we saw it, and reported it, and in essence signed the death warrant for the drug."

Though some trepidation remained in the management offices in Groton, the value of the Central Research structure was proven in due time with the commercial launch of one of the most successful products in Pfizer's history. Invented at the Groton laboratory, carried through clinical trials in the U.S. and at Euroclin, and documented and registered by the registration departments in Sandwich and Groton, Feldene was a shining example of the collaborative projects Central Research could turn into winners. Up to that time, it was the biggest drug that Pfizer had ever seen, and it changed the company from a primarily antibiotic house to a major player in the area of chronic disease management. "There had been a sort of psychological hang-up with antibiotics – penicillin, Terramycin, tetracycline, Vibramycin," says John Niblack. "Everyone said, 'Antibiotics, that's Pfizer's thing,' and we didn't know whether we could make serious money in anything else. Feldene changed all that. In fact, if it hadn't come through, we might have gone under without its revenue to keep us alive."

Pfizer hit pay dirt with Feldene, but its scientists had to dig a long time to reach it. It started in 1962, when the company decided for the first time to assign a team of scientists to work on drugs for arthritis. Joe Lombardino, who already had five years experience at Pfizer as a medicinal chemist, was the lead chemist, and Ted Wiseman became the chief biologist on the project. The plan was to look for a new anti-inflammatory agent that was structurally novel and did not have the problems of existing drugs, which were of low potency and had to be taken three or four times a day. Some of the existing drugs were quite toxic as well.

Lombardino started designing and, together with Nelson Treadway and Paul Kelbaugh, began making

compounds. Four times they hit upon an interesting structural class of agents, only to be frustrated by their poor toleration in animals. By that time, five years had gone by with not a thing to show except negative results. Despite the frustration, the project pushed on to explore additional novel compounds. As a back-burner project, Lombardino began probing around potential arthritis drugs from a new, previously unknown structural class (4-hydroxy-1,2 benzothiazine-3-carboxamides) that later became known as the oxicams. There was no specific authorization to make these new chemicals and no project abstract that approved these types of molecules. Lombardino recalls the many synthesis failures that preceded the successful preparation of the key intermediate compound that led to the oxicam series. "I have often wondered what would be the consequences to Pfizer if we had stopped one experiment short of success," he says.

As structural modifications were made in the oxicam series – eventually many hundreds of compounds were made – the activity of these compounds in the animal models that Wiseman was running began to improve dramatically, and the company was interested in advancing the project into Phase II clinical trials to see whether an oxicam had any effect on arthritic patients. Just as the team was testing the first oxicam, coded CP-14,304, in patients and getting some interesting indications that it was actually working, Lombardino synthesized sudoxicam, CP-15,973. Its potency was so much greater in the animal models that they halted clinical work with CP-14,304 and substituted sudoxicam. Lombardino remembers his excitement when he learned from Wiseman how much more active sudoxicam was in animal models. "We achieved a level of potency I used to wish for only in my dreams," he says. Just as Wiseman's animal models predicted, very much smaller doses of sudoxicam were found to be active in arthritic patients.

"We were really high at that point," Lombardino remembers. "We thought we had accomplished all of our goals."

About a year into the earliest Phase III trials in 1972, however, just as sudoxicam was going into more and more arthritic patients, the team began to get reports of liver enzyme elevations, not unlike those one sees with viral hepatitis.

"We didn't know whether we had coincidental cases of hepatitis or whether indeed we had a drug that was toxic to the liver," says Wiseman. "There was evidence in France that blood transfusions to patients in the program might have

carried hepatitis B and that a physician in Arizona had worked in a Mexican foundling hospital where there had been an outbreak of hepatitis. Then a patient died in New York. It was uncertain whether, among her several medications, she had actually taken sudoxicam, but it was evident that we would end up for many years debating the point with the FDA."

Management was sharply divided over what direction to take. Some people argued that Pfizer should push on with sudoxicam. Others said it looked pretty bad; we need greater safety; we'll never be able to sell such a drug. Still others said, let's drop the oxicams and get out of the antiarthritic area, or look elsewhere and start all over again. "Looking back, I would say that the company's future financial health was teetering right there," Lombardino observes.

Fortunately, Lombardino already had another backup compound in the oxicam series coded CP-16,171, later named piroxicam, and it was decided after much debate to risk the additional expense of testing this new agent — even though it was years behind sudoxicam in development — rather than risk continuing development of sudoxicam, which might be perceived as an unsafe drug. Piroxicam turned out to

Piroxicam, trademarked Feldene, is Pfizer's groundbreaking anti-inflammatory drug. It took 20 years of research and development before FDA approval in 1982, just in time to support Pfizer's move to greater research expenditures. It became one of the leading agents against arthritis.

have no liver problem; it was just as potent and could be taken only once a day. It combined the high biological activity and safety that the program had long been seeking. But it took still more years of development, mainly gathering extensive clinical data, before it was finally approved for marketing first in Switzerland in 1979 and eventually in the United States in 1982 – thus requiring a total of 20 years from the start of the project. The project involved the synthesis of hundreds of compounds and the expenditure of tens of millions of dollars. They were years of alternating frustration and excitement for the scientists involved, but such is the nature of research. "People have asked me what kept me going for all those frustrating years," says Joe Lombardino. "My answer – the hope of reaching the ultimate goal of finding a new medicine that actually helps patients."

Piroxicam received the trademark Feldene. The Marketing Department had tested a series of computer-generated names on panels of physicians and found that it was the most memorable name.

"The name didn't mean anything or have relevance to anything," says Lombardino. "It has meant billions of dollars in sales for the company since it was launched. Sales of the drug carried the company through the 1980s. It has also brought relief from pain and suffering for

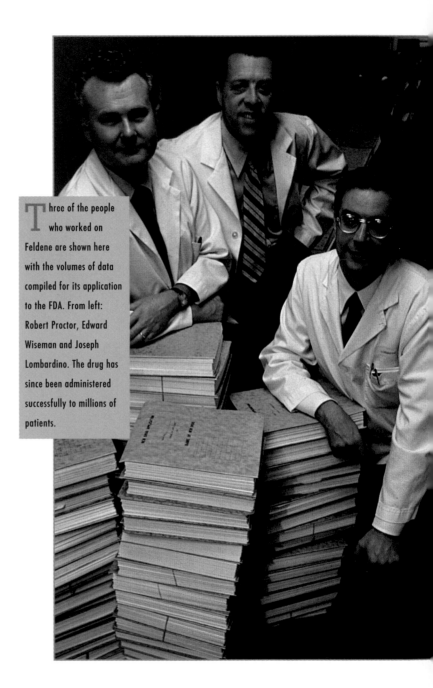

Three of the people who worked on Feldene are shown here with the volumes of data compiled for its application to the FDA. From left: Robert Proctor, Edward Wiseman and Joseph Lombardino. The drug has since been administered successfully to millions of patients.

tens of millions of patients, some of whom I have had the pleasure of personally meeting. That was my greatest reward – shaking hands with a grateful patient who said, 'Thanks for Feldene. It has improved my life tremendously,'" says Lombardino.

In the early 1980s, Sidney Wolfe of the Ralph Nader group mounted a challenge to Feldene, charging that it had more side-effect potential than Pfizer was letting on and arguing that something ought to be done to limit its use drastically. Pfizer fought that battle for years, with ultimate success; the FDA took no regulatory

10 years of patent protection from the time of its U.S. launch; when it went off patent in 1992, generic competitors were immediately introduced. By the end of that year, Feldene had lost almost half its U.S. market share to imitative products produced at lower cost by companies that did not bear the costs of the 20-year research and development program that produced Feldene.

But it was great while it lasted. Thus, it seems appropriate that Building 118W at Groton Central Research, built with reinvested Feldene profits, is now the site of Research executive headquarters. Despite the

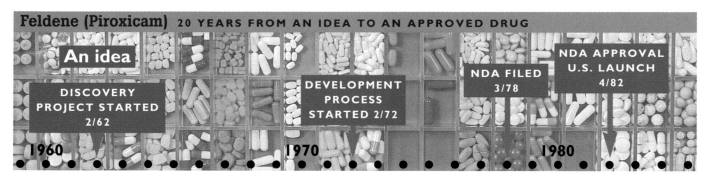

Feldene (Piroxicam) 20 YEARS FROM AN IDEA TO AN APPROVED DRUG

An idea

DISCOVERY PROJECT STARTED 2/62

DEVELOPMENT PROCESS STARTED 2/72

NDA FILED 3/78

NDA APPROVAL U.S. LAUNCH 4/82

1960   1970   1980

action. But the accusation was played up in the press and did its damage, cutting into Feldene usage. When Wolfe again challenged the safety of piroxicam in 1995, the FDA again rejected his arguments.

Nevertheless, Feldene became one of the world's leading antiarthritic agents and one of Pfizer's largest-selling products for almost a decade. It enjoyed only

initial hesitancy of Pfizer management, the decision to create a unified Central Research paid off. The coordination and direction it supplied to Pfizer's research was an important ingredient in the drug discovery and development process and thus in building the company's stature and presence worldwide.

"It was a very exciting time – going all over the world, seeing countries in various stages of development and deciding whether Pfizer should go in and how great an investment we should make. I just loved it. By 1959, nearly 85 percent of the company's profits came from International."

In 1964, Powers went to McKeen once more, indicating his desire to retire at the age of 50 and go on to other things. McKeen asked him as a favor to delay his re-

John J. Powers, Jr.

Jack Powers, former chairman, president and CEO of Pfizer, died April 12, 1994 at the age of 81.

Powers – whose father had been with Pfizer since 1909 and was vice president of sales until 1945 – graduated from Yale Law School in 1937, joined Pfizer as its first general counsel in 1941 and was involved in the company's wartime work in developing penicillin, the product that brought Pfizer into the emerging field of modern pharmaceuticals. The success of a subsequent antibiotic, Terramycin, introduced in 1950, was in good measure attributable to Powers, who used the worldwide demand for it to fuel Pfizer's rapid expansion into a global organi-

zation. He was named chairman of the company's international operations in 1955.

He recalled that Pfizer got into the international business almost by accident. "One day I was reading the annual report of Squibb, which reported that they had 35 percent of their sales in international trade and that was producing nearly 55 percent of their profits," said Powers. "I walked down the hall into the office of John McKeen, who was then Pfizer's chairman and CEO, and said 'John, look at this.' He said, 'Well, it looks as though we ought to go ahead.' I said, 'The only problem I can see is who are you going to have run such a thing – a big international trade outfit?' He said, 'You.'

tirement by a year to take over the restructuring of both Pfizer's research and its domestic pharmaceuticals business.

"During the course of this year, I noticed one young fellow who always seemed

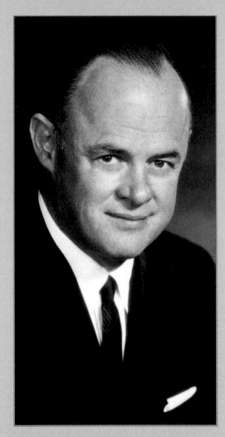

By the time Powers was named president and CEO of Pfizer Inc in 1965, the company's products were being sold in more than 100 countries, and it was clear that its research was moving ahead with a broad new vision. He succeeded John McKeen as chairman of the board in 1968.

Heavily involved with Pfizer's expansion into a multinational pharmaceutical company, John Powers served as Pfizer's chief executive officer from 1965 to 1972. During that time, the company's sales nearly doubled, passing the billion-dollar mark.

During his years as CEO, from 1965 to 1972, Pfizer's worldwide sales and profits nearly doubled, with sales passing the billion-dollar level in December 1972.

"Jack was a valued and respected colleague," says Ed Pratt, now Pfizer chairman emeritus and Powers' successor as chairman in 1972. "His passing leaves an empty place in our lives and our hearts."

to come up with an answer when other people were stumped," he said. "Because he had such good explanations of what was going on, I became increasingly interested in him. That was Gerry Laubach." Laubach was made head of the Research Division in Groton. The new objectives he set for the company's global efforts in medical research became the foundations of today's Central Research Division.

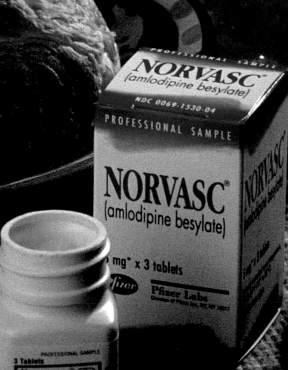

NORVASC™
(amlodipine besylate)

NDC 0069-1530-04

PROFESSIONAL SAMPLE

NORVASC®
(amlodipine besylate)

5 mg* x 3 tablets

Pfizer
Pfizer Labs
Division of Pfizer Inc., NY, NY 10017

PROFESSIONAL SAMPLE

3 Tablets
Norvasc® 5
(amlodipine besylate)

5 mg*

Pfizer Labs
Division of Pfizer Inc., NY, NY 10017

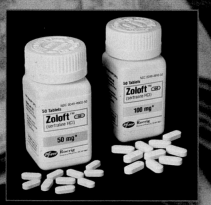

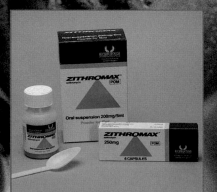

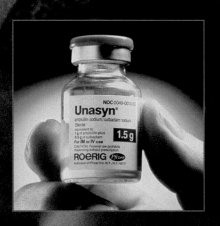

4

Increased expenditures for research produced several success stories for Pfizer in the 1980s. Products of these boom years included Norvasc, a calcium channel blocker given once a day for both angina and hypertension; Zoloft, a once-a-day agent for depression; Zithromax, an oral antibiotic for skin and respiratory infections; and Unasyn, an injectable antibiotic for specific mixed infections.

CHAPTER FOUR
Boom Times

"You are profitable in pharmaceuticals only if you innovate," says Ed Pratt, Pfizer's chairman of the board from 1972 to 1992.

To back up his belief, Pfizer spent almost $6 billion on research and development during his tenure, challenged the giants of the industry and produced a series of innovative medicines that impressed both the medical world and Wall Street. Company revenues grew from $1 billion to $7 billion. Pfizer stock began a climb that produced one of the highest appreciation rates in the industry.

"In the 1980s, I pushed Central Research and our pharmaceuticals group to grow even faster than they might have wanted to," says Pratt. "It was our only choice if we were to be numbered among the world's leaders."

The inspiration for this rapid explosion of sales and financial support for Central Research was Feldene.

Pratt had remained supportive of the work being done in the 1970s, but the proof of Central Research's potential was in the pudding. It wasn't until Feldene that a large increase in funding and the subsequent growth of Central Research was deemed a wise step.

Says John Niblack: "We were very successful with Feldene, and people began to look at the size of Pfizer R&D versus the other major companies and say, 'We can't battle against these other guys with a force that is one-third or one-half the size of theirs. If we're going to play in the majors, we're going to have to invest in R&D.' And so we hired hundreds of scientists and built up our labs in Groton and Sandwich and later in Japan."

One who disagreed with the rapid expansion was Gerry Laubach, then the company's president. Ian Wrigley remembers a favorite analogy of Laubach's: "Research organizations are like plants; they should be nurtured with great care from seed, or they will rapidly die." Laubach cited other companies, like Merck, that had expanded rapidly and then gone through a period when they had to lay off research people and endure a series of painful reorganizations. He wanted a lean organization for long-term stability and success.

"He was afraid that if we grew too fast, we'd be sticking our necks out. That was a valid concern," says Ed Pratt. "I was inclined to be more optimistic, but we

A 1992 aerial view of Central Research headquarters in Groton, Connecticut, shows the growth that the boom years made possible. In the background are the Pfizer manufacturing plant and the Thames River.

always listened to Gerry's views because they were always carefully thought out. We could play it close to the vest and try to be careful not to lose. I wanted to play it more aggressively and play to win, and we have won. Right now, we're the most highly regarded pharmaceutical company in the world — as far as our prospects for the future are concerned — because we have more meaningful products coming out of research."

And so there was the odd situation of Gerry Laubach, the former research director, resisting rapid growth in research, and Ed Pratt, the accountant and former company comptroller, urging it. In the end, Pratt prevailed.

In 1971, research and development expenditures totaled $38 million, and worldwide research staff amounted to 1,047 people; in 1981, those figures came to $179 million and 1,583 people. It wasn't until Feldene that such a large increase in funding, enabling the subsequent growth of Central Research, was deemed a wise step. By 1991, sales and staffing figures had risen dramatically to $757 million and 3,060 people, and in 1994 to $1.1 billion and 4,280 people – almost a 29-fold increase in dollars and a four-fold increase in personnel since Central Research was founded.

As the scientific force grew by leaps and bounds, there had to be a way of keeping senior management abreast of the exploding new drug-discovery activity. One of the most successful innovations of the last decade was the formation of a senior research management committee in 1983 to keep tabs on the increasing number of discovery projects being worked on in Central Research. The brainchild of Walt Moreland, then head of U.S. Research, and John Niblack, then director of research for Medicinal Products, with Barry Bloom's strong support, it brought together for the first time in a definite structure the various directors of

Discovery research at Groton and Sandwich and, later, Nagoya. It has become what Bloom terms "probably the most sophisticated system for self-appraisal of any American pharmaceutical company."

"We discuss research goals on a yearly basis," says Charles Harbert, now vice president for Development Planning. "We review longer-term strategy, experiments in how to do things, how we're doing relative to our own expectations and to the competition. From that, we develop new strategies and new approaches and define new experiments we'd like to try."

Then came the idea of Project Operating Plans, also suggested by John Niblack, which includes the process by which Pfizer reviews all of its discovery efforts on a yearly basis and determines whether or not each is progressing at an appropriate pace. Moreland initiated an analysis of survival statistics of experimental drugs. Since the attrition of compounds in development is so high, Discovery has to keep taking "shots on goal" – adding to the number of development projects – to keep the pipeline full. This effort was strengthened through the concept of Core Groups, scientists dedicated for the long term to working in areas where there are recognized major medical needs and opportunities.

After little more than a year in that job, he got a call from General J. Lawton ("Lightning Joe") Collins, a war hero and former army chief of staff who was serving as a board member and consultant to Pfizer, and who was looking to hire away some of Defense Secretary Robert McNamara's "Whiz Kids." In 1964, Jack Powers signed him on as Pfizer's controller – even though he wasn't one of the "whiz kids."

Edmund T. Pratt, Jr.

Ed Pratt grew up in Elkton, Maryland, where he developed a "consuming interest in almost everything." He swam, fished, hunted, boated and learned how to play football, baseball, tennis and golf. He earned money through high school and college playing the trumpet and briefly considered it as a career. In 1947, he graduated from Duke University (courtesy of the navy V-12 program) with a degree in electrical engineering and followed this in 1949 with an MBA from the Wharton School of Finance.

Fresh out of Wharton in 1949, Pratt joined IBM as a salesman, rooming in Endicott, New York, during a training program with John Opel, who went on to head IBM (and to serve on Pfizer's board for 20 years). After marrying Jinny, a young lady he had known at Wharton, he was called back by

the navy for the Korean War, spending two years as an officer at the Charleston Naval Base before rejoining IBM and moving to New York as administrative assistant to the executive vice president of IBM. He later became budget director and then controller of IBM World Trade in 1958. In 1962, at the age of 35, he took leave from IBM to join the Kennedy administration as assistant secretary of the army for finance, the equivalent of a four-star general.

Before long, Powers was considering Pratt as a potential successor to the job of CEO. Said Powers: "I realized he was a very intelligent and hardworking man, but as time went on I was increasingly impressed with other attributes – his directness and honesty, and also his ability to get along with people. He was very loyal. He might debate something with you, argue about it, but once the decision was made he would faithfully execute it."

A major test of Pratt's loyalty came in 1967, when Powers asked him to join Pfizer International to coordinate its activities with those of the domestic company. He accepted, despite the strained atmosphere in International, caused in part by a rather fierce insistence on independence from the parent corporation. Pratt immediately set out to learn all he could, traveling widely to visit the facilities and meet the people of Pfizer International. He was named president of International two years later. He wouldn't be long in that role either: he became executive vice president of Pfizer Inc in 1970, president of Pfizer in 1971 and chairman and chief executive officer in 1972.

At the same time, Gerald Laubach, who unlike Pratt had been with the company for 22 years, rising from head of Research to chief of Pfizer's pharmaceutical business, was named as president.

"I took every opportunity to make it clear that we shared the leadership," Pratt recalls. "He always worked well with me, although our personalities were almost opposite. He must have felt a grave mistake had been made in choosing me instead of him. He said as much, and I would have felt that way, too, if I'd been in his position. However, we made it work for 20 years, without much sparks or tension, until we both retired, and that's an accomplishment considering how different we are. We were able to lead Pfizer together because we had the long-term interest of the company in mind and were willing to sublimate our own feelings to that end."

"One of Gerry's roles, a role I could never play and yet an important one, was that of the man who can always spot potential problems," he adds. "He saw a boogey-

Edmund T. Pratt, Jr., Pfizer's former chairman of the board who advocated rapid expansion of Pfizer's R&D. Far left, he is pictured at a farewell party at Sandwich, England. He accepts the Queen's Award, below, for Technological Achievement with Alan Wilson, Sandwich's former research chief.

man behind every tree, and for some reason there were a lot of trees."

One point on which Laubach and Pratt differed was the need for pouring more money into research. In 1972, Pfizer hit $1 billion in sales, yet was spending less than 5 percent of that, $44 million, on research. Pratt felt that percentage should grow as fast as reasonably possible, even if it meant a reduction in profits. The magic number was between 15 and 20 percent, and Pratt pushed research to maintain that rate of growth, despite Laubach's conservatism. Says Pratt: "I had a lot of confidence in the research people and in Gerry himself, and it turned out to be well-founded."

Ed Pratt was Pfizer's CEO for nearly 20 years, an extraordinary reign. "I never expected to stay that long – in principle, it was too long," he says. "The success of the

company, personal success and monetary rewards have all meant a great deal to me. But what has meant the most is the outstanding support that I've received from Pfizer people. The feeling of a leader who is followed with warmth and enthusiasm is a marvelous feeling. That has been the greatest reward of my career."

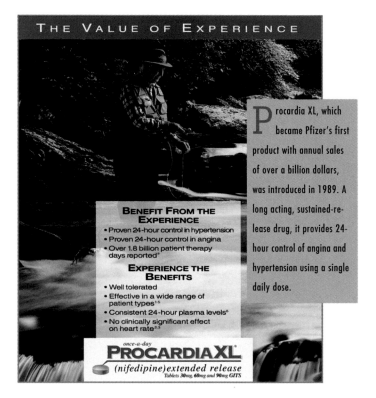

THE VALUE OF EXPERIENCE

Procardia XL, which became Pfizer's first product with annual sales of over a billion dollars, was introduced in 1989. A long acting, sustained-release drug, it provides 24-hour control of angina and hypertension using a single daily dose.

BENEFIT FROM THE EXPERIENCE
- Proven 24-hour control in hypertension
- Proven 24-hour control in angina
- Over 1.8 billion patient therapy days reported*

EXPERIENCE THE BENEFITS
- Well tolerated
- Effective in a wide range of patient types[1-5]
- Consistent 24-hour plasma levels[6]
- No clinically significant effect on heart rate[2,3]

once-a-day
PROCARDIA XL
(nifedipine) extended release
Tablets 30mg, 60mg and 90mg GITS

In 1986 a Development Management Group, consisting of seven senior managers drawn from each of the line functions was formed to monitor development candidates in the pipeline; the same year, the formation of cross-departmental Early Candidate Management Teams for managing drug candidates was initiated under the leadership of Joe Lombardino.

The use of regular management meetings (e.g., the Development Management Group, and the Quarterly Development Review) was started in the mid-1980s and helped Central Research to continuously examine itself. The use of metrics and tracking systems made a true science of research and development. For example, by modeling attrition rates in development, calculations could be made on what Discovery needed to deliver in order to attain corporate output goals for new pharmaceuticals.

During the early 1980s, Pfizer's drug development pipeline really started to perk. It was this new attention to the focus and organization of R&D that enabled Pfizer to develop so many successful products in laboratories across the globe. After a decade of transition, a new productive atmosphere had developed at Central Research.

The first antifungal drug from Sandwich's research, Trosyl (tioconazole) was approved for marketing in the United Kingdom and Germany in 1981. Since it was the first product in many years for Sandwich, it was a major morale-booster. That same year there were 56 new drug candidates from Sandwich and Groton in clinical development in Europe, and Euroclin had more than 200 clinical trials in progress, a number that increased to 450 the next year. In 1982, Pfizer licensed Procardia (nifedipine) from the German firm Bayer. This agent was introduced into the U.S. market for the treatment of angina, a widespread ailment affecting 2.5 million Americans. Angina manifests as chest pain and may be caused by clogged arteries, coronary artery spasm or a combination of both. Dosed three times a day, Procardia provides effective relief from angina with minimal side effects.

Although Procardia was the top drug in its class, it was still deficient in some ways: it was not approved for the treatment of hypertension, a disease that many angina patients have concurrently; it did not provide a prolonged presence of active drug in the blood, especially in the early morning hours when attacks of angina are more prevalent; and it needed to be taken three times a day, an inconvenience for patients that often leads to poor compliance.

Procardia XL, using a unique, patented controlled-release delivery system, addressed all these deficiencies. A product of high-science technology developed by the Alza Corporation, the new formulation was selected for licensing by Pfizer from several available slow-release formulations. It produces a long-acting, sustained release of drug that provides 24-hour control of both angina and hypertension using a single daily dose. Introduced in 1989, the XL formulation took an excellent product and made it even better. Patient acceptance was so high that Procardia XL went on to become Pfizer's first product with annual sales of a billion dollars.

In 1983 pirbuterol, a drug for asthma that was discovered by Wayne Barth in Groton, was licensed to 3M Pharmaceuticals in the U.S. where it is sold as Maxair.

Simon Campbell, one of the company's research directors at Sandwich, is among the discoverers of Cardura, an important antihypertensive. This and other contributions in the cardiovascular area earned him the Royal Society of Chemistry's prestigious Award in Medicinal Chemistry.

Cardura (doxazosin mesylate), an alpha blocker used as an antihypertensive, was discovered in Sandwich by Simon Campbell and others; it was approved in 1987 and launched in the U.K. in 1988 and in the U.S. in early 1991. Extensive trials involving more than 4,000 patients showed Cardura to be highly effective with a low incidence of side effects. Unlike many other antihypertensives that work through the kidney, brain or heart, Cardura gradually causes relaxation of the smooth muscle in the vascular system, thereby reducing blood pressure. Cardura is a widely prescribed antihypertensive around the world today, with steadily increasing market share.

Sulprostone, a prostaglandin discovered by the team of Jasjit Bindra, Tom Schaaf, Ross Johnson, Jim Eggler and Hans Hess, was licensed to Schering AG, who now sells it as Nalador.

The Growth of Sandwich

Central Research at Sandwich was definitely booming. Part of the reason was the presence of Alan Wilson, who took over from Ian Wrigley as head of Research in 1986 and kept the position until 1992, when he was succeeded by Peter Ringrose. Wilson brought a wealth of experience to Pfizer and helped to complete the Norvasc and Diflucan programs begun earlier. After earn-ing a medical degree and a Ph.D. in pharmacology, he had spent five years with the Wyeth Division of American Home Products, then worked on new drug regulation for the Committee on Safety of Medicines (CSM), Britain's equivalent of the FDA. He had also been medical director of the U.K. Trade Association and an independent consultant before joining Pfizer in 1980.

Wilson's background with regulatory agencies was a tremendous asset when he joined Pfizer. His first assignment was to run the newly formed Clinical Regulatory Affairs Group (CRAG). There was a need to make better use of the data that were being generated in the preclinical and clinical programs in order to put the best package together for registration. The first package CRAG put together was for tioconazole, an antifungal that was the forerunner of Diflucan. Then it got involved in working on Feldene when that drug was making its mark on the global market. Feldene was being challenged, but CRAG was able to keep the issues in perspective.

"At the time I took over from Ian, clinical programs were getting dramatically larger," recalls Wilson. "It became evident that we were going to have to expand, and so we put forward a proposal for opening up

Alan Wilson, former senior vice president of medicinal research and development, Europe, and Barry Bloom, Pfizer's former executive vice president for Research and Development, tour the newly constructed addition to the Sandwich facility.

the West Site, on the other side of the road from where the production plant and earlier research buildings had been. There was to be a new clinical research building, a headquarters building, a Discovery building, an Animal Sciences building and a Pharmaceutical Development building. All told, it came to nearly half a million square feet of new construction, at a total cost of more than £200 million [roughly $300 million], a very substantial investment.

"No corporation would have sanctioned that sort of expenditure on a group that had not shown that it could produce the goods. Unlike other U.S. companies, Pfizer now has an organization that in Europe can do everything, from discovery through development to filing, and that can collaborate with Groton as part of a transatlantic team. We have produced world-leading drugs in Diflucan, Cardura and Norvasc. Other companies don't give that level of independence to their European subsidiaries."

Pfizer Expands In Japan

To enable Pfizer to benefit from the talents of Japanese scientists, to enhance its relationship with the academic and regulatory communities in Japan and to make Pfizer Taito more comparable to major Japanese pharmaceutical companies, it was decided in 1983 to expand the Central Research operation at Taketoyo. Since 1972, Taketoyo had functioned as a microbiology laboratory searching among soil samples for new antibiotics and for new anti-infectives for Animal Health. The manager was Junsuke Tone, who had a staff of about 28 people. With the advent of new product patent laws in Japan, it made sense to establish a discovery unit focusing on synthetic chemistry and pharmacology. Hans-Jurgen Hess, former vice president of Medicinal Products Research, now retired, was put in charge of setting up the new unit. Authorization was given in 1983 for an initial group of 25 people; the labs in Taketoyo were opened in June 1985.

Critical for success, and representing a key challenge, was recruitment of a qualified Japanese manager, who was to assume responsibility for the new group and the microbial screening group as well. Says Hess: "There was a reluctance on the part of qualified Japanese people with an established record of accomplishment to join foreign-based companies, which had a reputation of hire and fire. Personal contacts, networking, appropriate

A researcher at Pfizer's labs in Nagoya, Japan, compares slides of tissue cultures on a light box. The research group at Nagoya seeks new leads for drugs from microorganisms and also specializes in discovery of agents for inflammatory diseases as well as analgesics for treating pain.

letters of introduction from famous professors and a lot of hard work and patience were needed to gain credibility." In 1985, Hess was able to hire Yoshihiko Kitaura, a manager from Fujisawa, one of the larger Japanese-based pharmaceutical companies. Kitaura, now executive director of Pfizer Central Research Japan, is also a board member of Pfizer Japan. He was later joined in the management of Central Research operations by Atsushi Nagahisa, manager of Medicinal Biology; Masami Nakane, manager of Medicinal Chemistry; and Nakao Kojima, manager of Natural Products Lead Discovery (microbial screening).

Today the research group in Nagoya (actually Taketoyo) numbers roughly 100 highly educated, professional people, who, in addition to seeking new medicinal leads from microorganisms for discovery projects worldwide, operate powerful research teams involved in the discovery of drugs for inflammatory diseases, primarily arthritis and asthma, as well as analgesics for treating pain. Important contributions of the microbial screening group enabled the discovery and development of Aviax (semduramicin), which is approved in the United States as an antiparasitic for chickens. The microorganism which produced Aviax in a screening technique developed in Nagoya was initially isolated from fermentation of a soil sample collected in Kyushu, Japan.

There is no question that Pfizer Japan is now capable of discovering new drugs: by 1994, the laboratory had five candidates ("CJ" compounds) in the development pipeline and four more ready to enter development.

Part of the reason for Pfizer's success in Japan is

the Japan Planning Committee, which was started in 1989. Meeting twice a year – once in Japan and once either in Groton or Sandwich – the committee is chaired by Ken Wolski, executive vice president, Japan R&D, and includes senior managers from Central Research, the International Pharmaceuticals Group and Pfizer Japan.

Prior to the Japan Planning Committee, Central Research would not transfer drug candidates to Japan for their development until after a compound had established safety and efficacy and had gone through three or four years of safety and clinical testing – which then had to be laboriously repeated to satisfy Japanese regulatory requirements. Japan is the second largest market for drugs in the world, however, and Pfizer was missing a valuable opportunity by getting to that market much later than it needed to.

The committee decided to step up the pace by getting candidates to Japan at a much earlier stage in their life cycle, by presenting the entire dossier of candidates to the Japanese and asking them which candidates would be especially useful in their market. Since the candidates were still so early in development, some of them inevitably failed, a new experience for the Japanese scientists. It became apparent that there was not sufficient expertise within the Japanese operation to deal with the problems posed by early candidates. So in 1991, John Henderson, with 16 years of experience working with clinical studies in Europe, was asked to go to Japan to head development operations and to provide that expertise. He stayed for two and a half years, building and strengthening the organization and establishing a network of contacts, and he brought this knowledge along when he transferred to Pfizer's New York headquarters.

Successes and Disappointments In the 1980s and 1990s

Pfizer's worldwide research team was harvesting an impressive series of successes in the 1980s, but even boom times are not exempt from heartbreakers. Sorbinil was one of them.

Scientists had long been intrigued by the fact that diabetics die young, usually of a cardiovascular disease. These patients all show changes in the eye, either retinitis or some opacity in the lens, and they all exhibit a deterioration of the peripheral sensory system, going numb in their fingers or toes. Researchers hypothesized that all these apparently disconnected effects were caused by a defect in an enzyme called aldose reductase. The enzyme normally transforms glucose to fructose, which can be handled by the body, but when levels of glucose get very high, as in diabetic patients, the enzyme transforms glucose to sorbitol, which cannot escape body cells and therefore accumulates.

In such cases the cells swell up like balloons and burst. If the cells happen to be in the retina, a person goes blind; if they happen to be in the descending aorta, a person has a major cardiovascular accident; if they happen to be in the peripheral nervous system, a person loses sensation and begins to experience tingling, pain and weakness in the extremities.

In 1976, Pfizer researchers, including chemist Reinhard Sarges, found a regulator of the aldose reductase enzyme, one that was very potent, had a long duration of action and was well tolerated in animals. They later named it sorbinil. The problem was how to study it in man.

"It turned out that our physicians and our scientific apparatus builders came up with an extremely clever innovation to measure something called motor nerve conduction velocity," says Ted Wiseman. "When you put out your hand and touch something hot, you immediately pull it back. You can measure the speed of that reaction by putting sensors at two positions along the nerve and finding out how long the message takes to make the journey. In diabetics, because of their damaged peripheral sensory system, it takes longer. We could then treat the patient with sorbinil and watch the motor nerve conduction velocity come back towards normal."

Pfizer embarked on an ambitious program with the National Eye Institute of the National Institutes of

Health, which recruited diabetologists and screened patients. Pfizer provided the drug at no charge and provided measuring technology and computer backup to assess the results. Things were moving along wonderfully. Physicians were telling Pfizer that their patients' peripheral nervous systems and their eyesight were beginning to improve.

Then disaster struck. The program encountered three patients who had a massive hypersensitivity response to sorbinil – three out of thousands. So in 1988 sorbinil studies were stopped, and a program was started to find a new drug," remembers Wiseman.

In 1994 Pfizer scientists found some structurally different inhibitors of aldose reductase; these are now being evaluated in human studies, about six years after the company dropped sorbinil. The most promising is a carboxylic acid called zopolrestat, which has gone through Phase II work. It has been found to improve peripheral nerve function substantially and, happily, doesn't have any hypersensitivity problem so far.

Sorbinil might have met an impassable roadblock, but other drugs were moving full speed ahead. In 1987, the Roerig Division of Pfizer Pharmaceuticals (named for a company Pfizer had taken over in 1953 as its first major acquisition) launched a new product for hospital use – Unasyn, an injectable antibiotic for specific mixed infections. Along with the broad-spectrum antibiotic Cefobid and the antidiabetic Glucotrol, it was the third new product for Roerig in five years.

The Unasyn story began in 1970 when James Retsema, manager of Infectious Disease Research at Groton, formed a team to work on an improved version of Geocillin, an antibacterial which is ineffective against certain resistant strains of bacteria. Between 1970 and 1974, the chemistry team, led by Tim Cronin, synthesized hundreds of beta-lactam compounds, none of which amounted to much. Though they couldn't find an improved version, Cronin's leadership of beta-lactam chemistry research helped develop a clearer picture of what they were looking for. In late 1975, they started to seek an inhibitor of beta-lactamase, a bacteria-produced enzyme that renders Geocillin and many other penicillin antibiotics ineffective.

In July 1976, Wayne Barth, a research advisor in the Medicinal Chemistry Department at Groton, synthesized sulbactam, which, after extensive laboratory testing, proved to be an efficient beta-lactamase inhibitor. At this point, the team discovered that sulbactam and ampicillin, a widely used antibiotic, were synergistic – they worked well together against many important ampicillin-resis-

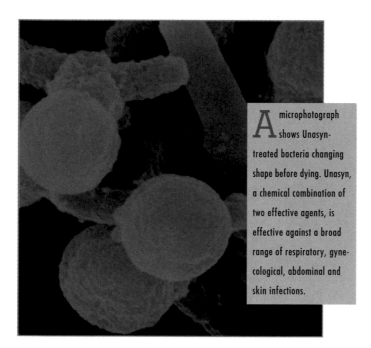

A microphotograph shows Unasyn-treated bacteria changing shape before dying. Unasyn, a chemical combination of two effective agents, is effective against a broad range of respiratory, gynecological, abdominal and skin infections.

tant bacteria. When combined in one drug, sulbactam inhibits the beta-lactamase enzyme, clearing the way for ampicillin to attack the infection-causing bacteria. Unasyn takes its name from this phenomenon: one drug ("una") that results from the synergy ("syn") of two.

Following 10 laborious years of development, the FDA approved Unasyn for use in the United States in December 1986. Prior to launch, it was tested in 150 hospital microbiology laboratories to demonstrate how it performed against bacteria commonly found in hospitals. At the time of its marketing, it was the only beta-lactamase inhibitor indicated for gynecological

infections, a leading cause of infertility in women in the United States.

In 1992, Pfizer hit the jackpot with the unprecedented launch of three major new products in the United States:

• Zoloft (sertraline), developed at Groton and launched in February, soon became one of the most successful antidepressive medications in history, rivaling the highly touted Prozac. Zoloft is one of a new class of agents for the treatment of depression. It does not have a long-lasting metabolite like Prozac and is taken just once a day, a great convenience for the patient.

• Zithromax (azithromycin), developed at Groton and launched in March, was the first of the azalides, a new class of antibiotics that works with the body's natural defenses at the site of infection. It combines the shortest course of therapy with a comprehensive spectrum of activity against infectious organisms. Zithromax promises to become one of the most important oral antibiotics ever marketed, especially in pediatric patients, for whom a pleasant-tasting liquid form has been developed and approved for marketing.

• Norvasc (amlodipine besylate), developed at Sandwich and launched in November, is the first of a new generation of calcium channel blockers that can be given once a day for treating both angina and hypertension. It stays at a nearly constant level in the blood through 24 hours, including the important early morning hours when cardiovascular attacks often occur, and is well tolerated. Norvasc promises to become the largest-selling Pfizer drug of all time.

Of these three superdrugs, Zithromax is an especially interesting case study, and illustrates how laborious and fraught with obstacles drug development can be. From beginning to end, it took no less than 18 years to bring to market. The story starts back in 1974, when Pfizer scientists at Groton began working in the area of macrolides, which at the time was on "the cutting edge of chemistry," according to Frank Sciavolino, then director of Natural Products Research and leader of the research team.

"Big-time academic people like Robert Woodward and E. J. Corey, both at Harvard – the premier leaders in organic chemistry in the world – were trying to synthesize macrolides," says Sciavolino. "It was not a program where we had a clear shot at anything; we were really setting out on a path that was unexplored."

Macrolides, the class of antibiotics that included erythromycin – originally marketed in 1952 – were the only existing naturally occurring antibiotics that had not led to a second-generation product. Tetracycline had led to doxycycline, penicillin to amoxicillin, but ery-

thromycin had produced no heir. The problem with erythromycin was that it was unstable in stomach acid, and a lot of it was rapidly degraded. The products of degradation caused side effects in the small intestine, increasing the rate of peristalsis and causing pain. Another problem with erythromycin was its spectrum of activity; it was ineffective against a major pathogen called hemophilus influenza.

So the team set about trying to make a better erythromycin. As the program proceeded, they made well over 2,000 compounds between 1974 and 1981 – a substantial program for Pfizer at the time. Of those 2,000, 13 compounds were advanced into toxicology studies, and 8 of those went into human trials. What the team was looking for was a compound that would produce blood levels two to four times higher than erythromycin. They didn't see it.

"The majority of compounds we were working with were chemical modifications of one of the sugar components of erythromycin, but this didn't translate into higher blood levels," says Sciavolino. "So we started working on a different portion of the molecule, and some interesting relationships between structure and activity began to emerge. By changing a ketone into an amine, we found that we dramatically increased the acid stability of the compound. We also found that if we compressed a certain portion of the molecule the potency against hemophilus influenza also increased."

Around that time, the Groton researchers noted that scientists at Pliva Pharmaceuticals in Zagreb, Yugoslavia, had applied for a patent on an interesting new macrolide compound that was very close to what they were doing. Resynthesized by Jim Hauske and Gloria Kostek as CP-60,273, it was found to have a unique, expanded antimicrobial spectrum. The problem was that it was inactive by the oral route — a crucial attribute for a marketable drug.

Mike Bright, a research chemist, was assigned the task of investigating ways to build oral activity into the compound. On March 20, 1982, after some nine months of labor, Bright and his colleague Dick Watrous made a key change in what they called the "Seattle" (upper left) region of the molecule, blocking the "Bangor" (upper right) region with oxygen so that a CH3 group would light on Seattle instead of Bangor. The resulting compound was orally active, acid-stable and effective against hemophilus.

"There's a lot of luck in this business," says Bright. "Sometimes there's only one thing that will work, one key that will unlock the door. That turned out to be the magic one." What Bright and Watrous had created had the mind-boggling chemical name of (2R,3S,4R,5R,8R,

10R,11R,12S,13S,14R)-13-[(2,6-dideoxy-3-C-methyl-3-O-methyl-*a-L-ribo*-hexopyranosyl) oxy]-2-ethyl-3,4, 10-trihydroxy-3,5,6,8,10,12, 14-heptamethyl-11-[[3,4,6-trideoxy-3-(dimethylamino)-ß-*D-xylo*-hexopyranosyl] oxy] -1-oxa-6 -azacyclopentadecan - 15-one. In simpler terms it, was compound CP-62,993 – azithromycin.

Just as the research effort was turning the corner, Pfizer was seriously considering shutting down the eight-year program for lack of results. At what was to be their last quarterly review meeting, the team presented information on CP-62,993. John Niblack, for one, thought it was right on the money, but other managers questioned the wisdom of pushing on.

"We were within a rat's hair of pulling the plug," says Frank Sciavolino.

"At the eleventh hour, the cavalry arrived," says Mike Bright.

In toxicology studies, azithromycin displayed respectable blood levels in laboratory animals, but when it was tried out in humans, researchers found that blood levels were one-tenth of that predicted — a puzzling and disappointing result. At the time, the conventional wisdom said that an effective antibiotic had to have blood levels about four times higher than the MIC, jargon for the Minimum Inhibitory Concentration that is necessary to kill a microorganism.

"Because they couldn't measure enough antibiotic in the blood, they were ready to chuck it out the window," recalls Scott Hopkins, group director of Clinical Research. "But it worked so well in infected animals that they knew something very good must be going on. They went back and measured the concentrations in tissue, in living cells, and found the drug was there in enormous quantities. That certainly perked up interest."

What this proved was that azithromycin moved rapidly into tissues – lung, liver, spleen, muscle – which are the actual sites of most infections. Not only was it widely distributed in tissue; it was also present in white blood cells that normally travel to the site of an infection to kill the bacteria that are causing it. "It is really a very targeted kind of delivery, a phenomenal one," says Sciavolino. "We're not aware of any other drugs that work by this mechanism."

However, the Zithromax team had not yet successfully navigated all the hurdles. During this time, Pfizer was not the only company seeking oral activity for the drug. The Pliva scientists credited with the invention of the earlier CP-60,273, had been seeking a solution to the same problem of oral inactivity. Pliva's independent efforts had also been successful, and the company sought a patent for the new compound outside the U.S. Thus,

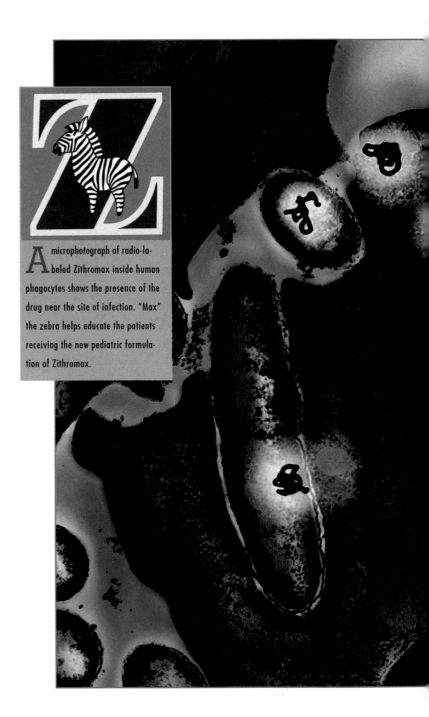

A microphotograph of radio-labeled Zithromax inside human phagocytes shows the presence of the drug near the site of infection. "Max" the zebra helps educate the patients receiving the new pediatric formulation of Zithromax.

while the Pfizer team independently discovered azithromycin, Pliva's scientists are the legal and rightful inventors.

It was not until the U.S. government issued Pliva an equivalent patent that Pfizer determined that CP-62,993, for which Pfizer had already received a U.S. patent, was the same compound that had also been patented by Pliva. ("We both had U.S. patents on the same compound, which was an oversight on the part of the U.S. Patent Office," observes Sciavolino.) Because the overlap had been unavoidable on either company's part and because Pliva's patent indicated that their discovery had predated the discovery of the same compound at Pfizer, a co-marketing partnership agreement was worked out whereby Pfizer would abandon its patent in return for rights to market the drug throughout most of the world, while Pliva would sell in the Eastern Bloc countries, including Russia.

Azithromycin, given the trade name Zithromax, was finally introduced in 1991 in the United Kingdom and elsewhere overseas and in the United States in 1992. It is considered a milestone in antibiotics. Unlike other antibiotics, which must be taken three or four times a day for seven to 14 days because they leave the body quickly, its affinity for infected tissue makes it powerful and persistent enough to do the job when prescribed only once a day for five days. Whereas up to 82 percent of patients on a multi-dose, multi-day schedule forget to take their medicine, such noncompliance was observed in less than 1 percent of the 4,000 patients studied for Zithromax's New Drug Application.

Prescribed mainly by primary-care physicians, to whom most people turn when they have a sore throat, ear infection or skin infection, Zithromax is also being used by pulmonary specialists and ear-nose-throat specialists against such afflictions as chronic bronchitis and asthma. The new drug is also extremely effective against *Chlamydia trachomatis* infections, the most common sexually transmitted disease in the United States – where some 4

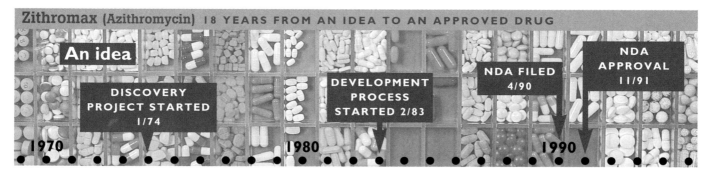

Zithromax (Azithromycin) 18 YEARS FROM AN IDEA TO AN APPROVED DRUG

An idea

DISCOVERY PROJECT STARTED 1/74

DEVELOPMENT PROCESS STARTED 2/83

NDA FILED 4/90

NDA APPROVAL 11/91

1970   1980   1990

million cases are treated annually – and in the rest of the world, where it is the major cause of blindness. A single one-gram oral dose is as effective as the standard regimen of 14 doses of doxycycline.

The market for Zithromax could become even larger as clinical studies continue. Pediatric studies have applied it to two common childhood ailments – otitis media, an ear infection, and streptoccocal pharyngitis, a throat inflammation – as well as acute sinusitis. "We believe that Zithromax works especially well with children," says Scott Hopkins, "because parents find it difficult enough to give medicine to kids twice a day, let alone three or four times a day for a week to 10 days. Zithromax, given once a day, is a blessing for them." The NDA for the Zithromax pediatric formulation was approved in October 1995.

Says Gary Jortner, vice president and general manager of Pfizer Laboratories: "Zithromax has everything required to be a breakthrough drug. The antibiotic market will now be defined as pre- and post-Zithromax."

Another interesting example of the discovery and development of a major drug is the story of Norvasc (amlodipine). Roger Burges, a biologist by training and now director of Development Planning at Sandwich, was the team leader in the discovery of Norvasc, a member of a class of drugs called calcium channel blockers originally developed to treat angina. The first calcium channel blocker (CCB) was described in the 1960s, and in the late 1970s Pfizer acquired the license to market a new one, Procardia, in the United States. Despite Procardia's success, the company didn't have a drug available to market to the rest of the world. The research group in Sandwich was charged with finding a new CCB that had advantages over Procardia and that could be marketed worldwide.

The project, which began in 1979, examined Procardia and other existing drugs to figure out how to improve on them. It was clear what the deficiencies were. First of all, the drugs had to be taken three times a day. They also had a high level of side effects, producing dizziness, facial flushing and headaches.

The objective was to get a drug that overcame these side effects by being absorbed more slowly and lasting longer so it could be taken once a day. "We didn't honestly believe at the time that we could do it," says Burges. "But in drug discovery you have to set yourself a target. One important thing in our favor was that we had at Sandwich a dedicated drug metabolism group that studied the kinetics of the drugs in animals. This enabled us to get rapid feedback on whether a new compound actually did last longer in animals."

The discovery team decided to make substitutions on a place in the molecule that was originally thought to be impossible to derivatize. It took two years and 1,500 compounds to discover amlodipine, as the agent came to be called. It was first synthesized in 1981, and clinical testing in man took place from 1982 until 1987, about five years – a fairly rapid program considering the fact that the drug was being developed for two large indications, hypertension as well as angina. The

launched in Japan, the number one market for calcium channel blockers, and Germany, the third largest market after the U.S.

Tenidap represents still another example of a major R&D program. In late 1993, Pfizer submitted a New Drug Application for tenidap, an antiarthritic drug. The NDA – the largest ever compiled by Pfizer, if not the largest ever submitted by any pharmaceutical company – was bigger than the NDAs for Zoloft, Norvasc, Diflucan and

Left, chemists who worked on the tenidap project which led to the largest NDA Pfizer ever submitted, stand in front of the mountain of paperwork it involved. From left are: Ralph Robinson, Larry Rieter, Joe Lombardino, Saul Kadin, Larry Melvin, Kelvin Cooper and Anthony Marfat. At right, Pfizer employees celebrate the send-off of the application to the FDA. Below, a large tenidap collage is on display at Pfizer's Groton facility. It is made up of hundreds of pictures of the people who were involved with the discovery and development of tenidap.

compound was given to about 2,500 patients and volunteers in the United States and Europe. The New Drug Application was submitted in December of 1987 and was finally approved by the FDA in 1992. In 1994 it was

Zithromax *combined*. It consisted of 1,200 volumes of data, each volume about 400 pages long – totaling three tons of documentation, a staggering load of paper. Even at that, it represented only some 40 to 50 percent of the information compiled on more than 10,000 subjects, which was summarized in tables. (The average NDA contains data on clinical trials of 2,000 to 3,000 subjects.) In a send-off ceremony at Groton, the cartons of volumes were loaded into a truck for the trip to the FDA offices in Rockville, Maryland. Sandwich, which supplied about 25 percent of the data through Euroclin, had filed an International Regulatory Dossier (IRD), the European equivalent of an NDA, for tenidap (called Enablex) earlier in 1993.

Tenidap was synthesized by Saul Kadin in Groton in 1983 as part of a large discovery effort that examined 2,400 chemical compounds in the oxindole structural class. Compound CP-66,248, later named tenidap, was chosen as the best development candidate. Bringing it to NDA status has involved the labors of nearly a thousand Central Research investigators and support staff over a 10-year period.

To protect the franchise established by Feldene, Pfizer had continued investing heavily in researching new approaches to inflammatory diseases, seeking not only to relieve symptoms such as pain and swelling but also to attack the causes of inflammation and joint destruction. After years of testing, Central Research believes that tenidap has this dual action. It not only relieves pain by inhibiting the production of prostaglandins, like other drugs, but it also blocks the action of cytokines, which stimulate the production of cartilage-degrading enzymes. Tenidap shows efficacy in rheumatoid arthritis and in the much more common osteoarthritis. This broad spectrum of activity, combined with the convenience of once-a-day oral dosing, gives tenidap the potential to replace many existing antiarthritic agents.

The extensive clinical program – some patients took tenidap for five years – was needed to document not only that the drug was active and safe, but that it was an improvement over existing therapies. Says Mike Leeming, clinical team leader for tenidap in Sandwich, "We believe we have conducted the largest and best designed studies ever performed of the effect of a drug on arthritis." Pfizer's action, in effect, raises the hurdle for other drug companies. Says John Niblack, "The large, detailed comparative studies exemplify the kind of NDA that the industry will be required to file more and more in the future."

marquis who had recently immigrated to France from Algeria.

"We first found that the roof was under repair, so a couple of members, including Peter Ringrose, had leaky tarpaulins over the top of their rooms. Junior members were assigned rooms over the adjoining stable, where those of us who had allergies were ill by the end of the week. The maid welcomed us by cutting a bar of soap into four pieces and handing each one of us a piece.

ing table, which were constantly replenished as mice ran back and forth on the beam above.

Barry Bloom's room boasted a huge, hairy spider, which used Bloom's tub as its private hunting ground. John Niblack's bathroom had no curtains, so when he was taking a shower, those who toured the castle could watch him; visiting Boy Scout and Girl Scout troops would walk by and wave.

The final indignity came on the last day

The Chateau de Gué Péan

The main meeting of the Discovery Management Committee alternates yearly between the United States and Europe, with members spending a working week to address strategic and tactical issues regarding Discovery. Undoubtedly the most memorable was the meeting held in 1984 at the Chateau de Gué Péan in the Loire Valley of France.

"It was just one disaster after another," recalls Chuck Harbert. "At the last minute, the date and site had to be changed. Since the new meeting date overlapped a major French holiday, the only place we could find was an old, run-down chateau owned by a

"The toilet in at least one room was so close to the wall you had to sit side-saddle. The pipes banged, so that every time someone flushed a toilet the whole building would shake. The walls were so thin that we could hear one of our number who was a loud snorer, so one of us took the responsibility for walking him up and down the hall until everyone else had gotten to sleep."

The room in which the group met was an old turret with stone walls and floors — cold, damp and dreary. There was only one chandelier, and the lights kept going out, leaving the members in the dark. There were mouse droppings each morning on the meet-

when Barry Bloom discovered his toilet kit was missing. It had apparently been stolen by one of the tourists. As a memento of this meeting, everyone got T-shirts inscribed, in French, "I survived the Chateau de Gué Péan." At the 10th anniversary DMC meeting, the Discovery Management Committee presented Barry with a new toilet kit and a rubber spider to commemorate the infamous trip.

the following day, having received his commission through ROTC. He served in the Third Armored Division in Germany from 1960 to 1963 as a tank platoon leader and was involved in the Berlin Wall crisis.

"The army was a good experience," he says. "For a while I thought of making it a career, but by the time I finished three years, I'd had enough of it and knew it wasn't for me."

He went back to school and studied bio-

Lloyd Conover, the discoverer of tetracycline and then director of chemotherapy research at Pfizer, came to the Illinois campus on a recruiting trip for new chemists. "I immediately liked Lloyd, the way he handled himself, the way he talked with me, and thought I'd like to work for people with that kind of respect for the individual. I was invited to Pfizer for an interview tour," says Niblack, who also interviewed at Merck, Lilly and DuPont. "I chose Pfizer primarily

John Niblack

John Niblack remembers well when, at the age of 18, he worked as a lab assistant in a summer job in the Standard Oil of New Jersey geochemistry labs in Tulsa, Oklahoma:

"I saw these guys with leather patches on their blazers. They came in about an hour later than anyone else, and they sat back in this room where they drank coffee and chatted with each other and the technicians. I said, 'Who are those guys?' And they said, 'Those are the Ph.D.s, the chief scientists who run the project.' That's when I knew for sure I wanted to get an advanced degree."

Niblack completed four years at Oklahoma State, majoring in chemistry. "By the time I finished, I was very tired of school," he says. He graduated one day in 1960, got married the next and went into the army

chemistry at the University of Illinois for four years, working on bacterial viruses and molecular biology. His Ph.D. dissertation was entitled "Host Suppression of Nonsense Mutations in Bacteriophage PF-1." His advisor was the chairman of the department, I. C. Gunsalus, who moved his laboratory to Cold Spring Harbor, Long Island, every summer. John's work at Illinois earned him a coveted spot on the laboratory's summer staff.

"The graduate students served as a kind of slave labor there," he says. "The hours were long and hard. But I was able to meet and actually work with some of the most famous biologists and molecular geneticists of the time, including many of the Nobel laureates such as Luria, Hershey, Watson and McClintock. It was a fabulous experience."

because, unlike the others, they said, 'Here's the problem that we're trying to solve. We'd like you to suggest how we might best solve it – what are your ideas.' I found that challenge very exciting and certainly very, very different from the way the other pharmaceutical companies seemed to operate. I think we've managed to maintain this philosophy as an element of our culture. We ask our new people to do a lot, and they are immediately participative and creative."

Adds Niblack: "I think I was Pfizer's first card-carrying molecular biologist. I'm not sure why they hired me, but I think it was probably perceived as fashionable to have a molecular biologist on the staff. Perhaps they thought they would hire one, and then eventually a use would be found for him."

Niblack's first assignment at Pfizer when he started in 1967 under Keith Jensen, head of Virology, was to work on new ways to induce the formation of the lymphokine interferon. His colleagues, Bill Hoffman and Jim Korst, found the first low-molecular-weight inducer CP-20,961, and Niblack organized its clinical exploration in a large series of controlled outpatient trials in the U.S. and Europe. "Although CP-20,961 failed to demonstrate in general use what it had shown in the trials," he says, "I learned a lot about the practical and scientific difficulties of clinical experimentation with conceptually new drugs."

In the early 1980s, Niblack extended the project abstract concept to include the reduction of discovery projects to one of several common denominators called "approaches," each of which has a certain life cycle and probability of success in various stages of development. Extending Walter Moreland's work on the historical success rates of Pfizer compounds, he developed unified concepts of the relationship between overall investment and output in R&D. These concepts led to a series of management tools and techniques that continue to underlie the management of Pfizer's discovery operations.

In 1986, Niblack finalized the matrix team concept at Pfizer by establishing a Development Planning Group. Early Candidate Management Teams (ECMTs), with members representing all key departments, were formed to plan for and monitor early drug candidates. Advanced Candidate Management Teams (ACMTs), including representatives from marketing and other commercial departments, were established to plan for and track drug candidates that were in late stages of development. These teams have made significant contributions to improving interdivisional understanding and to producing development plans that meet Pfizer's needs.

The year 1986 also saw the appointment of Niblack as executive vice president

of Central Research, overseeing the development of Diflucan, Norvasc, Zithromax, Zoloft, Cardura, tenidap and other important pharmaceutical products. In 1990, he was appointed president of the Central Research Division, at which time he was also made a vice president of Pfizer Inc.

In 1993, Niblack became Pfizer's executive vice president for Research and Development, responsible for Central Research as well as Licensing and Development, Quality Control and Regulatory Affairs. As executive vice president and the senior science officer of the corporation, he reports directly to Pfizer's chairman and chief executive officer.

John Niblack, executive vice president for Research and Development, is the senior science officer of Pfizer. He has brought a "team" approach to the development of new drug candidates, including the creation of Early and Advanced Candidate Management Teams (ECMTs and ACMTs), which nurture each new drug through the many stages of drug development.

CHAPTER FIVE
Joining the Biotech Revolution

Scientist Anne Schmidt of Neuroscience Research in Groton, Connecticut, uses a cell harvester to conduct a receptor-binding assay for possible antidepressant therapies. This new approach, called target preparation, is made possible by advances in genetic biology that allow human receptors to be "manufactured" in quantities large enough to use in testing for new drugs.

In recent years, Pfizer, along with the rest of the drug industry, has been experiencing a revolution. Called the "biotech revolution" or the "genetic revolution," this new direction in research followed from the unlocking of the DNA molecule's secrets and the subsequent growth of genetic technology.

"Access to isolated human genes has revolutionized the way we search for novel drugs today," says Alan Proctor, executive director of Cancer, Immunology and Infectious Diseases. "The majority of the discovery approaches in our current portfolio are based on genetic technology."

The DNA sequencing laboratories established at Groton and Sandwich combine robotics and automated instrumentation with sophisticated new software and computing power from a big Cray computer. These fa-

cilities can produce and analyze tens of thousands of pieces of raw DNA sequence data per day, which represents many months of effort with older, traditional methods.

Proctor recalls that when he joined Pfizer in the 1970s, the recombinant DNA revolution was just getting started with experiments at Stanford University. When he heard about the experiments, he recognized that something exciting had happened: the experimenters had found a way to isolate specific genes, cut them out from the 3 billion bits of DNA that exist in every cell and manipulate them by splicing them to other genes. Proctor saw the relevance of the technique to what Pfizer was asking him

I n the automated gene-sequencing laboratory at the Groton research center — one of the first to be established in the U.S. pharmaceutical industry — scientists can determine information encoded in disease-associated genes that can lead to identifying new therapeutic targets. In the background can be seen a DNA fragment modeled on a computer at a revolutionary pace. Opposite, a researcher collects sequencing data on a gene. Gene sequencing is in the forefront of drug discovery in the 1990s.

to do: to manipulate the organisms that were used in fermentation processes to make antibiotics.

In the early days of its development, however, the DNA revolution was embroiled in controversy. About six months after the biotech revolution got started, some of the scientists who had invented the new techniques began to get nervous that they might create some microbial monster that would escape into the environment and cause havoc. Thus, there was a self-imposed moratorium on recombinant DNA technology that lasted for a year and a half while the National Institutes of Health drew up research guidelines, which included identification and prohibition of the types of gene translocations that had the greatest theoretical potential to do harm to people.

Around 1976 the first of the biotech companies, Genentech, went public with a stock offering.

"The press made a big deal out of it," recalls Barry Bloom, "so that laymen reading the paper were convinced that cancer was within a few years of being cured. It was vastly overblown."

When the biotech industry started, it wasn't unusual for a professor with an idea to raise millions in venture capital overnight and develop a company that soon had a hundred people working on a product. "There

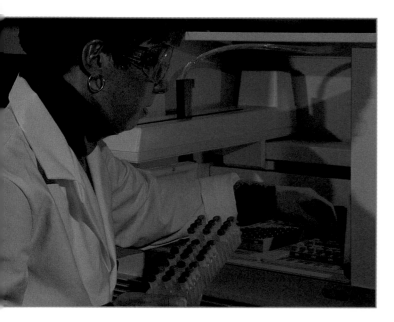

was always a lot of hype," says Alan Proctor. 'This is going to be a $2 billion dollar product' – that's what they said about TPA [tissue plasminogen activator]. The Pfizer projection was that TPA would probably be a $200-$300 million product. We were absolutely dead-on right. Genentech sold $243 million of TPA in 1993.

"A lot of the market projection was very unrealistic. In retrospect, the conservatism that gave us such a slow start was well founded. It kept us from building up a company to make protein products, which proved not to be the panacea that the biotech industry was hyping at the time.

"Many of our competitors had a knee-jerk reaction. Eli Lilly overnight hired 50 people to work on

molecular biology. It was frustrating to see our own company reacting very conservatively to this exciting new technology. While our entry into the field was more cautious, when we did go into it, we went in with a strategy that was very soundly focused on small-molecule discovery. Many of our competitors, having built up groups to go off and make protein products, had a hard time making that transition."

"There was a tremendous amount of faddism that was difficult to resist, but we did," says John Niblack. "The way that molecular genetics began to be used in the 1980s was to take a gene for a natural hormone, like insulin or growth hormone, and clone it, and put it in a microorganism and ferment the microorganism so that you were able to produce the hormone, instead of isolating it from animal or human organs.

"This didn't interest us very much because we felt that the number of such hormonal targets was small and that it was not an important area for meeting medical needs or for large commercial opportunities. We also believed that you couldn't get a patent on something like human growth hormone, which is a natural substance; you can only try to get a patent on the process by which it is made. Process patents are difficult to enforce because someone else can come up with a slightly different process that will achieve the same results. You could see during the summer of 1986 to discuss the value of these outside compounds and of random screening. In the fall he approached the then vice president of Research, Mike Page, and said he wanted to try this full time. Page thought the idea "a little goofy" but gave it the go-ahead anyway.

Vinick's small group, collaborating with John Williams and Dennis Pereira, the originators of high-throughput screening, set up three screens initially – for antagonists of

drug lead. For us it really was a break-through."

A whole world of novel drug discovery had opened up, but could they do it again? The group added more people and more sophisticated instrumentation so they would be able to screen compounds faster. "We stuck to our philosophy of bringing in novel potential therapeutic targets where there were no known active leads for drugs," Vinick says. "Many of these biological targets

Rapid Screening to Search

In 1985, Pfizer scientists began to worry that they were not finding enough drug leads in their library of compounds that were novel or distinct, that they were running into the same compounds over and over again. It occurred to Fred Vinick, then director of New Leads/Structural Chemistry, that the answer lay in bringing more compounds in from outside.

"I went off and did a deal – it was some-what unsponsored, a bit of a renegade operation – with the Aldrich Chemical Company," says Vinick. "It brought us our first outside compounds on an exclusive basis from various universities and other sources around the world."

Vinick also started meeting with other chemists and pharmacologists over lunch

substance P, a putative pain neurotransmitter; for neurotensin antagonists, which had possibilities for antipsychotic activity; and for cholecystokinin antagonists, which were thought to have interesting properties in the central nervous system. They set up assays using radio-labeled ligands binding to receptors on membranes to see if they could find compounds that would disrupt this binding.

The miracle took place in the area of substance P, where Kelly Porter Longo had screened about 700 compounds at what was then the extraordinary rate of 25 compounds a week. She found a substance P antagonist, one small chemical modification away from an eventual clinical candidate. Says Vinick, "It was a compound that we had purchased, a very interesting, potent

were classical hormone, neurotransmitter or enzyme systems that had been known for many years but had never been explored in a drug discovery program. In that sense, they represented an exciting, unexploited source of potential new drugs. It was a real chance to get away from following the competitors' leads – a real chance for break-through drugs."

In 1987 the group started going full bore. Screening evolved from handfuls of compounds to tens of thousands of compounds. Thanks largely to Robin Spencer, manager of Exploratory Medicinal Chemistry, New Leads brought the screening to a new level of sophistication – among the first in the industry and arguably the best. Spencer set up high-throughput instrumentation with the aid of robots and computers. The capability has since exploded to the point where the group can screen 50,000 compounds a week. New Leads continued to buy more compounds from outside. By 1993 its purchases had grown from 6,000 to the unprecedented level of more than 100,000 compounds a year.

Julie Olson, who is the current director, figures that about 75 percent of what her group does actually generates good leads that are worth the efforts of the other chemists,

for New Drug Leads

who then modify the molecules to get better results. It can take 100,000 compounds to find one decent lead, so the more compounds they test, the higher are the chances of success. Among those who have gone on to become drug candidates are the substance P antagonists, the CRH (corticotropin-releasing hormone) antagonists and the dopamine D4 antagonists. Other programs are moving rapidly toward candidate nomination.

New Leads, has almost single-handedly changed the drug portfolio balance of Pfizer from compounds that were fairly analogous to existing drugs to a two-to-one preponderance of structurally unprecedented drugs.

complications in the patent law immediately, and the last 15 years are replete with examples of lawsuits, infringements and contests of patents in this area."

Back when these arguments were going on, however, Pfizer's board would occasionally get very frustrated with the research management because the company had such a small presence in the area. "Our own board became nervous that we weren't moving aggressively enough into this new field, that we weren't acquiring companies," Barry Bloom says. "We tried to tell them that they weren't reading the potential of this situation quite right. Yes, there were going to be biotechnology products that would be highly successful, but the real potential of this new science was its ability to empower the more traditional forms of drug-seeking so that they, in turn, would become vastly more effective. And that indeed is what has happened."

"We decided that the main use to which we would put molecular genetics would be to acquire new targets for conventional drug research and development. For example, if there is a receptor in the human brain that may be associated with depression, and you want to engineer a drug that will fit that receptor, you can use molecular genetics techniques to prepare quantities of the human receptor so you can use it in the laboratory to tailor-make drugs to fit the receptor.

"So we didn't build giant fermentation plants; we didn't jump out and try to manufacture hormones. Instead, we began to move more slowly, into the target preparation zone. Some people like Lilly make hormones and do good business with them. But the record shows, and will show in the future, that we're going to have many more commercial opportunities than they have ever had."

"We slowly built a very effective group that is well targeted today," says Proctor. "In the late 1980s, we had to run like crazy to catch up, but we now have a credible capability in the area, not the largest in the industry but perhaps the best focused. In the last few years, our Molecular Genetics and Protein Chemistry Department has gone from the smallest to the largest department of the Discovery operation."

One of the first problems tackled at Pfizer using recombinant DNA technology was renin. This enzyme is made in the kidney and initiates a cascade of events that ultimately control blood pressure. If a person has too much renin activity, he or she develops high blood pressure. Ten or twelve years ago, when Pfizer became interested in trying to find a drug to inhibit renin, scientists had no access to human renin because the body makes so little of it. Using animal renin wouldn't work in this case because there is a very important, if subtle,

In Groton's X-ray crystallography laboratory, an experimental compound in crystal form is bombarded with X-rays. The various refractions of the rays will give research scientists a picture of its molecular structure.

chemical properties, and that one could enhance that activity by changing the structure. Two Pfizer scientists, Jim McFarland at Groton and Mike Tute at Sandwich, embraced this technology and soon put Pfizer in the forefront of this discipline, called quantitative structure-activity relationships.

The next advance in rational drug design was visualizing the receptor or binding site for a drug. By purifying a receptor, crystallizing it and irradiating the crystals with X-rays, researchers are able to get an electron density map telling them where in space the atoms of the receptor are. Then, on a high-resolution graphics workstation, a medicinal chemist can examine how a drug binds to the receptor and can hypothesize how to modify the drug to produce more interactions between the drug and the receptor, which makes the drug more potent.

Dominy's department bought its first high-resolution computer graphics system in

Computer-Assisted Design of

Computer Applications, led by Beryl Dominy, is relatively small as departments go: there are only four Ph.D. scientists manning it in Groton, an equal number in Sandwich and a lone researcher in Japan. But the department has a giant effect on the design of new Pfizer drugs.

The idea of rational drug design started back in the 1960s, when Corwin Hansch of California's Pomona College discovered that one could predict the activity of a compound based upon its structural features and

Computational chemists in Groton analyze the shape of a molecule's three-dimensional structure on a work-station screen. From left are James Blake, James Rizzi and Scott Snedon.

1985, and now their workstations are linked with Central Research's Cray supercomputer and a midrange multiprocessor computer. "Computers enable you to visualize what a receptor looks like," says Dominy. "You can look at it with three-dimensional glasses and almost put your hands into the structure. You can then identify what atom types are in there, whether they're oxygen atoms or carbon atoms or nitrogen atoms, and what kind of atoms would be compati-

New Drugs

ble with the receptor and what kind of shape they would have to be. You can then present that data to a chemist in a way that he can be creative with it."

"When we discover an active compound, there is usually some problem with it," Dominy continues. "For example: it's not potent enough, it's not active in vivo, has some toxicity, and we need to get around that problem by modifying the compound. A chemist looking at the structure of these compounds bound to a receptor will get ideas about changes that could improve the fit between receptor and drug."

In the case of compounds that are too readily metabolized, rational drug design can be used to identify structural changes that

don't interfere with the drug binding to the receptor but make it more stable, enabling scientists to generate new drugs that don't have to be administered as frequently.

Dominy's department is working on many compounds, including anti-inflammatories, cancer agents and drugs to combat the diseases associated with diabetes. He looks forward to having more and more receptor structures that can be used for designing drugs in the future.

"The holy grail we are seeking is to be able to predict the three-dimensional 'fold' of a protein just from its amino acid sequence. If we can predict with a computer

Beryl Dominy, manager of Computer Applications, left, and Fred Vinick, formerly a director in Medicinal Chemistry, pause for a picture before continuing their discussion on computations generated by Pfizer's big Cray computer.

all the relationships of the atoms in a receptor, without having to experimentally determine the structure, that will be a real breakthrough."

difference between animal and human renin in terms of the molecular structure and how it acts in the body.

"We were stymied," recalls Alan Proctor. "So we decided to try this new approach – clone the gene – a process that took a couple of years at the time. We pulled the renin DNA out of human tissue-culture cells and put it into a different cell which would grow in a cultural medium under the control of a DNA element that would cause that cell to produce lots of the human enzyme.

"So we invented little cellular factories to make large quantities of this rare human protein renin, and we gave the purified enzyme to our chemists and biologists who were trying to develop an inhibitor. We now had many options not previously open to us: assays based on the human enzyme; the ability to screen large numbers of compounds in a search for leads; but most dramatically, the ability to model the structure of renin and 'see' how our lead inhibitors interacted at the atomic level. These insights, gained through use of state-of-the-art X-ray crystallographic studies, helped our chemists surmount many of the hurdles this tough problem presented. They really led Pfizer into the modern medicinal-chemistry paradigm known as structure-assisted drug design."

By using recombinant DNA techniques to replace selected genes, scientists can now transform microorgan-

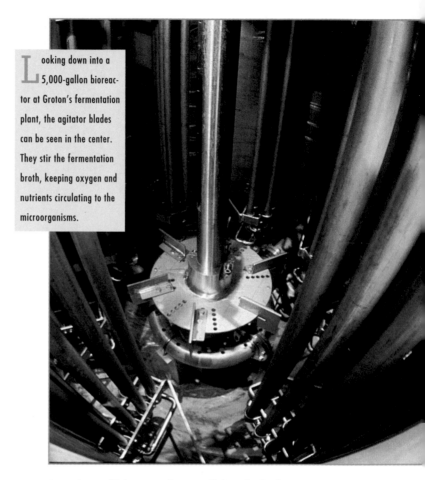

Looking down into a 5,000-gallon bioreactor at Groton's fermentation plant, the agitator blades can be seen in the center. They stir the fermentation broth, keeping oxygen and nutrients circulating to the microorganisms.

isms into efficient producers of chemicals that an organism would not normally make – a technical advance that has led to a resurgence of fermentation processing. Up to now, Pfizer's fermentation plants have been devoted largely to traditional, and relatively small, molecules, including two new animal health products, Aviax and Dectomax.

The first Pfizer product that took advantage of recombinant DNA technology and fermentation was an enzyme called chymosin – Chy-Max. "We learned a lot from chymosin, and we are beginning to apply that knowledge to medicinals," says Ken Taksen, executive director of Bioprocess R&D.

One of the most recent drug candidates to use DNA technology is insulinotropin, which is intended for use in the treatment of diabetes. Interestingly enough, Pfizer's molecular geneticists were able to take an organism that had been used long ago to make citric acid, a yeast called *Y. lipolytica*, and clone into it the genes that cause the organism to make insulinotropin at very high levels. Starting with that organism, Chris Strick's lab in Molecular Genetics was able to increase expression to levels unprecedented for recombinant yeasts, and then Taksen's group scaled that process up in a gleaming new pilot plant.

Taksen concludes: "The discipline of biotechnology can be a very important part of Pfizer's next century, as it was of Pfizer's first century. It's stimulating being both at the cutting edge of research and yet also part of that long-standing continuum."

Collaborative efforts have been a key strategy for Pfizer's participation in the biotech revolution, says Greg Gardiner, who, as group director of Research and Development Operations, oversees the company's collaboration with other companies and individuals. Since good ideas for new pharmaceutical products are not restricted to Pfizer scientists, the company seeks to tap into outside intellectual resources by a variety of means.

Pfizer began researching new biotech companies, and by the end of 1985 began making serious investments in some of them. The thrust behind these collaborations was that they would allow the biotech company to explore new areas of interest. Pfizer could get in quickly, invest further if the area proved productive and withdraw quickly if an area proved unproductive.

Pfizer's first biotech collaboration, with Oncogene Sciences of Garden City, New York, brought it into the area of cancer research. The five-year deal began in 1986 and was renewed in 1992. Pfizer built up its own in-house cancer group to work with Oncogene's when it became clear that further investment was warranted.

Gardiner says: "It has taken a long time to bear fruit because new approaches that will really change cancer therapy are finally beginning to get meaningful results. We've been setting up drug screens, and we've been getting drugs that are hitting some very important cancer targets."

The deals started to follow rapidly after Oncogene. In 1987 Pfizer signed an agreement with Natural Product Sciences of Salt Lake City, Utah, founded by two professors from the University of Utah, to work on spider venoms. Their theory is that toxins spiders use to paralyze, but not kill, their insect prey are likely to act in the human brain to protect neurons that usually degenerate in Alzheimer's disease or after a stroke. Though no new drug has yet resulted from the collaboration, it has turned up some interesting ideas, which Gardiner describes as "a real intellectual boost" to Pfizer's chemical research in the neurodegeneration area. Out of the collaboration have come some very important tools that allow Pfizer scientists to make drugs that selectively affect calcium levels in nerve tissue without affecting calcium levels in other areas like the heart, which could have serious consequences.

Among other collaborations, a major deal was struck by Pfizer's laboratories in Sandwich, England, with British Biotechnology of Oxford in the area of inflammation and atherosclerosis. Another collaboration, with Scios-Nova of Mountain View, California, helped produce insulinotropin.

As of June 1994, an agreement with Incyte Pharmaceuticals, Inc., of Palo Alto, California, gives Pfizer access to Incyte's library of gene sequences and high-throughput gene sequencing and analysis technology. The library contains what Incyte believes to be the world's largest compilation of profiles of gene expression by numerous cells and tissues, providing a detailed understanding of those genes that play pivotal roles in various human diseases. Central Research scientists send cells of special interest to Incyte for sequencing, analysis and correlation to biological phenomena – through comparison with Incyte's library – and then use the results for the discovery of novel targets for pharmaceutical intervention.

Collaborations were also established with non-biotech companies. In April 1994, an agreement was reached between Pfizer and Klinge Pharma of Munich, Germany, for the co-development of droloxifene, a drug that is active at estrogen receptors and has potential applications in the treatment and prevention of both breast cancer and osteoporosis.

From an agreement with Ligand Pharmaceuticals of San Diego have come new compounds that could be extremely useful in the treatment of osteoporosis.

A deal with Neurogen Corporation, a company founded in 1988 by Yale University scientists in Branford, Connecticut, involves the areas of anxiety, Alzheimer's disease and sleep disorders. Anxiety is the most common psychiatric disorder in the world. It affects 10 percent of the U.S. population, some 25 million people, and represents a $3 billion worldwide market for drugs.

Up to now, control of anxiety has depended on such widely used drugs as Valium and Xanax, which have enjoyed huge commercial success despite the incidence of various side effects ranging from sedation to tolerance, addiction, withdrawal symptoms, alcohol interaction, impaired motor skills and short-term memory loss. Moreover, many of these benzodiazepines were products of research three decades ago, leaving the anxiolytic market with nothing new in more than 20 years.

Through the collaborative effort with Neurogen – the largest of its type for Pfizer – Pfizer hopes to develop novel agents for treating anxiety. These agents bind very specifically to a subset of GABA (gamma aminobutyric acid) receptors, neurotransmitters in the brain that are implicated in anxiety, but they do not bind to the other subtypes that cause side effects. In the second year

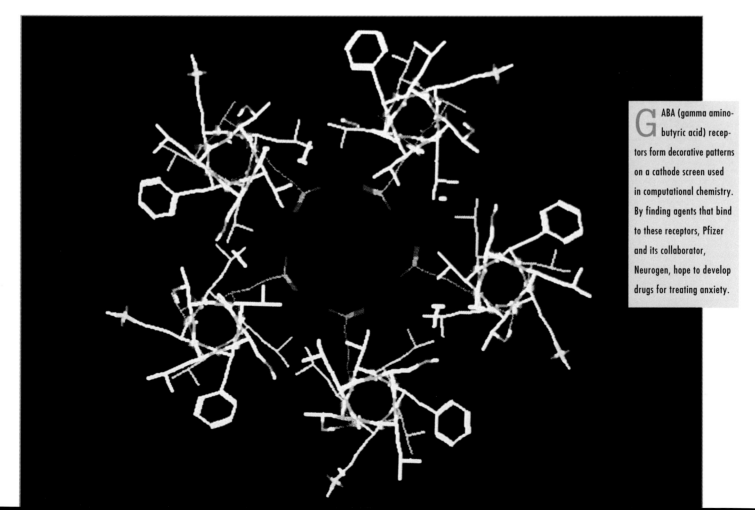

GABA (gamma aminobutyric acid) receptors form decorative patterns on a cathode screen used in computational chemistry. By finding agents that bind to these receptors, Pfizer and its collaborator, Neurogen, hope to develop drugs for treating anxiety.

of the partnership, the first drug entered clinical trials and was shown to be as effective as Valium in the treatment of anxiety but free of any sedative effect.

"We believe we have some drug candidates that represent the most promising new therapeutic approach to anxiety since Valium was introduced in the 1960s," says John Tallman, co-founder of Neurogen. Concludes Greg Gardiner, "Neurogen is one of the most successful investments we've ever made."

"Understanding the genetic foundation of human disease will be the foundation for new directions in pharmaceuticals," says George Milne, "We see the coming period as a time of unprecedented opportunity to make new therapeutic advances. Reflecting that conviction, we are augmenting our commitment by expanding both our internal efforts and external research collaborations."

These various ventures form a network of expertise in the emerging field of biotechnology that complements Pfizer's strength in the discovery and development of new drugs. The company has termed this network PfizerGen.

All in all, Pfizer has forged more than 20 of these collaborations, which are contracted to run from three to five years. Pfizer searches out a company that has a technological head start in an area of interest to Pfizer. One

example is Neurogen's work on anxiolytics. If Pfizer were to start the same research from scratch, it would probably take three to five years before the company could produce a candidate.

More recent collaborations have included ventures in the fields of gene therapy and microbial engineering, as well as two collaborations to help define the potential uses of drugs discovered through the efforts of PfizerGen companies. Immusol, a private company out of La Jolla, California, has made an agreement with Pfizer to undertake a five-year program to seek out potential ribozyme gene therapy for virus-spreading RNAs. The results of this collaboration would have a significant impact on treatment of viruses such as HIV.

Just as knowing the genetic map of the human body enables drug companies to determine how to target their drug therapies, knowing the genetic map of a fungal or microbial disease enables drug companies to better inhibit fungal infections, some of which, like cryptococcal meningitis, can be life-threatening. A four-year agreement with Myco Pharmaceuticals, Inc., located in Cambridge, Massachusetts, will help Pfizer stay on the forefront of emerging antifungal drug discovery.

In order to reap the full potential of new discoveries in the biotechnology field, Pfizer has teamed up with

AEA Technology, a U.K. government-owned business, to develop improved techniques for determining the function of new discoveries. By examining the role of particular genes in the body, this technology aids the search for new drugs by locating potential gene targets. Pfizer is getting some help in the development process as well. An agreement the company has signed with Oxford Assymetry, a privately funded company in the U.K., gives Pfizer access to "chemical libraries" of compounds to test for potential new drugs. This resource, along with the speed and efficiency of computerized, robot-driven tests enables Pfizer to increase greatly its probability of finding new drugs.

In addition to collaborations with other companies, Pfizer enters into contracts with many university professors who are doing research that is of interest to the company; for example, to produce certain cell lines or antibodies or animal models that Pfizer wants to use in research. Such contracts exist with scientists at Rockefeller University, Duke University and the University of California at Irvine in the United States. In the United Kingdom, relationships exist with Cambridge University, the University of Dundee and Kent University.

These collaborations help bring Pfizer to the technology front line. Never was there a question of Pfizer's enthusiastic pursuit of biotechnology, and what might have been initially perceived as reluctance is now acknowledged as just another example of Pfizer's commitment to following none but its own example – a commitment that has made Pfizer a pioneer in many respects. Barry Bloom explains the advantage Pfizer has gained: "What you see at Pfizer now is not a biotechnology department or a biotechnology project but rather the information and techniques of biotechnology diffused throughout the entire research program, making things feasible that weren't before, and making the discovery processes vastly more efficient."

Central Research, through its R&D Operations Department, now headed by Barrie Hesp, has also participated in the process of recommending and evaluating important drugs that could be licensed from other companies. For example, in an agreement signed with Eisai, a new drug called Donepezil, or E-2020, an agent commonly regarded as the best for the treatment of Alzheimer's Disease, has completed clinical trials and is being prepared for registration.

These vials and dishes of plants and herbs could have been in an apothecary's collection of remedies years ago. Recently, these remedies of old have been combined with modern science to begin a collaboration which could produce many new drugs.

A New-Old Approach: Drugs

Gene splicing is not the only new approach developed with the help of modern technology. Computer-aided analysis of complex structures is enabling scientists to examine the chemical composition of plant extracts as well.

Pfizer, under the leadership of George Milne, has entered into a $2 million, three-year agreement with the New York Botanical Garden to produce plant extracts that might have medicinal value. In the first year, the search is concentrating on a broad sampling of plants from around the United States; collections in the second and third years will focus on plant varieties that are known to produce medicinal compounds or that have been used as folk remedies in other cultures.

The samples are prepared for analysis in the New York Botanical Garden's laboratory, then sent to Groton where they are screened for pharmacological activity by members of the Natural Products Group under Gary Schulte, the scientist heading up the project for Pfizer. A major obstacle to working with plants in the past was the ex-

could be useful in the treatment of organ-transplant rejection and autoimmune diseases such as rheumatoid arthritis.

As part of this project, Pfizer and the Academy of Traditional Chinese Medicine in Beijing have begun a three-year collaboration focused on the potential pharmaceutical uses of Chinese medicines. The idea of researching folk remedies and plant extracts is not new. Many companies have begun analysis along these lines. However, tradi-

One quarter of all prescription drugs originate from plant life, yet less than 1 percent of the estimated 250,000 species of flowering plants worldwide have been analyzed for possible use in human therapy. Says George Milne: "I expect this collaboration to lead to substantial advances both in research and in our understanding of the importance of biodiversity."

From Plants

treme difficulty of separating the many components in a plant extract, a process that would often take years. New technology now enables the laboratory to process hundreds of extracts a week — each containing thousands of components — without separating the components unless an extract is active in a screen. The extracts are taken to biological screening, where their effect is tested for potential use against dozens of diseases, including cancers, autoimmune disorders, diabetes, bacterial infections and heart disease. Already, the lab has found a family of promising compounds extracted from plants used by Native Americans that

tional Chinese medicine has been practiced for centuries, and thus gives Pfizer's venture a firm foundation from which to conduct their research effort. Not only are Chinese plant extracts being examined, extracts from the United States and its territories are also being researched.

The advocate behind this research collaboration is biochemist Ting Po I, a research advisor at Pfizer who orchestrated the deal. This agreement is also advantageous for Pfizer in the area of new markets. China is a growing market which will become more familiar and more accessible to Pfizer as a result of this project.

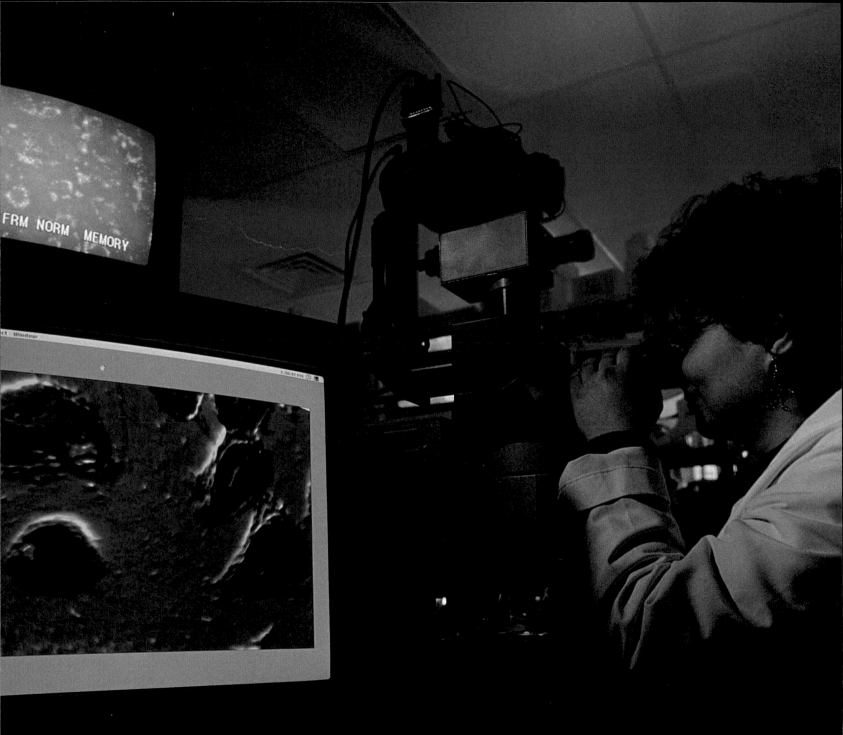

6

CHAPTER SIX

Turning Prototypes Into Prescribable Drugs

Drug discovery involves the use of many technologies. Here Kristina Rafidi in the Cancer Research Group lab in Groton uses image analysis to get a closer look at flourescently labeled human cells.

W hen a promising new drug candidate has been discovered, Development takes over to establish its safety and efficacy and – if a myriad of hurdles can be overcome – eventually get it to market. Getting a drug to market requires a seemingly endless obstacle course of tests, phases, teams and data – and a little bit of luck.

When the Discovery scientists working with research compounds (the "R" of R&D) reach a point where they think they have a chemical worthy of further development (the "D" of R&D), they write a document called Candidate Alert Notice (CAN) asking management to allow them to take the drug into the development process.

Approval of the CAN leads to the creation of an Early Candidate Management Team, an ECMT, a system Pfizer has had in place since the 1980s. This team brings together the key individuals from the 10-12 specialty departments who must work together to efficiently develop the drug candidate. The Development Planning Group, formed in Groton with Joseph Lombardino as its head in 1986, provides full-time project coordinators to work with the ECMTs. Initially, nine ECMTs were formed in Groton, from which one new product, Zithromax, has emerged so far.

The ECMT is chaired by an individual who is deemed to be the best qualified to champion the drug, often the person who worked closely with the drug candidate during the discovery phase. The team also includes representatives from the Early Clinical Research Group and the Clinical Research Department, which will be testing the drug in humans; representatives from the Metabolism Department; Developmental Research; Drug Regulatory Affairs (the people who will be dealing with the Food and Drug Administration); Safety Evaluation; a scientist or two from Discovery; and a project coordinator from Development Planning. They work together as a team whose main goal is to plan ahead and to get the candidate over the many obstacles that lie in its path.

The same team system is used at Sandwich with a Development Planning Department under Roger Burges, who has been director of Development Planning there since 1989. Burges points out that the project champion (team leader) may have a lot of other research responsibilities and therefore cannot be a full-time team leader. This led to the concept of giving him a right-hand man, a project coordinator who does the detailed planning and the day-to-day coordinating of activities.

"In the end," says Burges, "what we're trying to do is get the drug registered in the shortest possible time. Time is money. After all, six months earlier onto the market with a billion-dollar drug is worth half a billion dollars!"

The newly nominated drug development candidate faces several phases of research: preclinical testing (such as safety evaluation and formulation research) and the clinical trials, labeled I, II, and III, in humans. Each of these clinical phases is progressively longer, more expensive and uses increasing numbers of subjects in the trials. Attrition of drug candidates takes place at every phase of the development research process. For the few research compounds that get through Phase I clinical testing, in which the drug is given to healthy volunteers, and Phase II, in which a drug is given to patients who actually have the disease at which the drug is targeted, a key decision point is reached.

When it is felt that there is enough information on the few surviving drug candidates to warrant large-scale Phase III studies, an "R2D2" – a Research Review for Full Development Decision – is issued. It contains safety and efficacy data on the patients studied in Phase I and Phase II; a prediction of what Clinical Research thinks the likely outcome will be when Phase III is expanded to thousands of patients; what medical profile the drug is likely to have; the cost of the remaining research; an analysis of how long it will probably take to get the drug to market; and what can be said about the drug vis-à-vis other existing drugs, including those competitors likely to be in the marketplace four to six years from now. The U.S. and International Pharmaceutical Groups can then do some market research of their own and offer their projections of the commercial valuation of the agent.

With approval of the R2D2, the ECMTs are replaced by ACMTs, Advance Candidate Management Teams. Some team members transfer from ECMT to ACMT: those from Discovery, Developmental Research and Drug Regulatory Affairs, as well as the project coordinator. The key at this stage is the addition of Marketing people, who will be in on development of an overall strategy for development, the design of Phase III trials and the target indications for the drug — the finished product and its labeling. The chairman of the ACMT, in fact, is a marketing person.

"We want Marketing to help plan the development of a drug so they will be entirely satisfied with the result," says Lombardino. "They know the competition,

An Advanced Candidate Management Team meets to discuss a candidate drug. ACMTs meet regularly throughout the development of a new drug and include team members from many different departments including Discovery, Developmental Research, Drug Regulatory Affairs and Marketing.

they know what they will be up against, they know what they'll be facing when they reach the marketplace. We need to satisfy their needs to the extent allowable by the science involved.

"It's worked out pretty well," says Lombardino, who established the ACMT system in 1987. "The strengths of the ACMTs are that they bring together the various key disciplines, the people who in the past would each be working in their own little sphere and passing information on. These people now come together; they're made

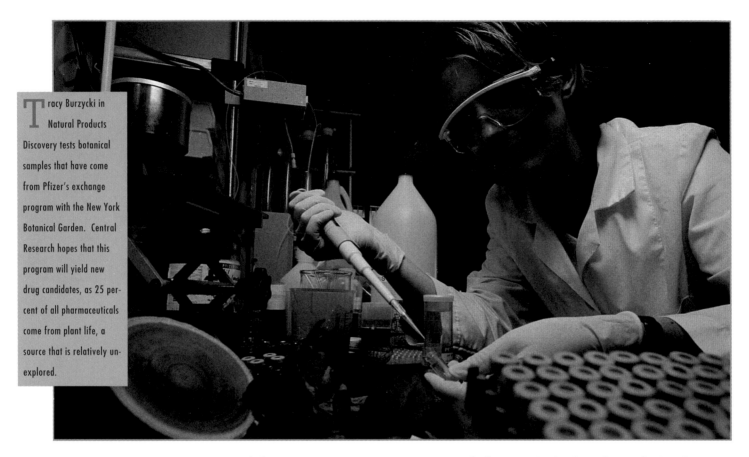

Tracy Burzycki in Natural Products Discovery tests botanical samples that have come from Pfizer's exchange program with the New York Botanical Garden. Central Research hopes that this program will yield new drug candidates, as 25 percent of all pharmaceuticals come from plant life, a source that is relatively unexplored.

to understand that this drug is their baby, so that the co-operation you see is much, much better than it used to be. Team members also learn about the problems of others on the team, leading to mutual understanding and respect for each other. Now you've got 10 or more good brains tackling the problem. A good team chairman will solicit opinions from everyone, not just the expert in a particular area; often someone else will come up with a good idea with a fresh twist. In the end, a much larger

group of Pfizer people clearly understand what the new drug really is, what it can and cannot do, thus facilitating the development and marketing of the drug."

With all the emphasis throughout the 1980s on the "end game" of getting late-stage drugs ready for regulatory approval, near the decade's end it was apparent that greater quality investment in *early* stage candidates was needed to bring the next generation of new products forward.

Early Clinical Research Group

Says Craig Saxton, now executive vice president of Central Research: "With the best intentions in the world, the division had been putting its resources behind late-stage candidates because that's what corporate management in New York was banging the table for. Final development (i.e. Phase III) is a highly complex, logistic game with a lot of moving parts, very heavy expense, a lot of people involved, a lot of data being collected. The rules of the game are largely dictated by regulation, including how data are analyzed, presented and filed with the FDA and other international regulatory agencies. The trouble was that all this was being done at the expense of the early development candidates that came out of

Discovery. They weren't getting the kind of attention they needed."

Only a fraction (less than 10 percent) of the drugs that enter into development ever make it out the other end of the pipeline, so it is important to identify as early as possible those that are most likely to make it and discard those that won't. The answer, in late 1988, was the formation of the Early Clinical Research Group (ECRG). This department, consisting of Clinical Pharmacology and Experimental Medicine, was charged with giving nascent drugs their constant, dedicated attention through Phase I and early Phase II, under the auspices of the Early Candidate Management Teams. In other words, they plan and carry out the earliest experiments in humans, the point at which critical "go or no-go" decisions are made on drug candidates.

From the archives, this picture shows Colin Taylor, left, cardiovascular research physician, and Craig Saxton discussing improvements in chest X-ray findings in a heart-failure patient receiving Minipress.

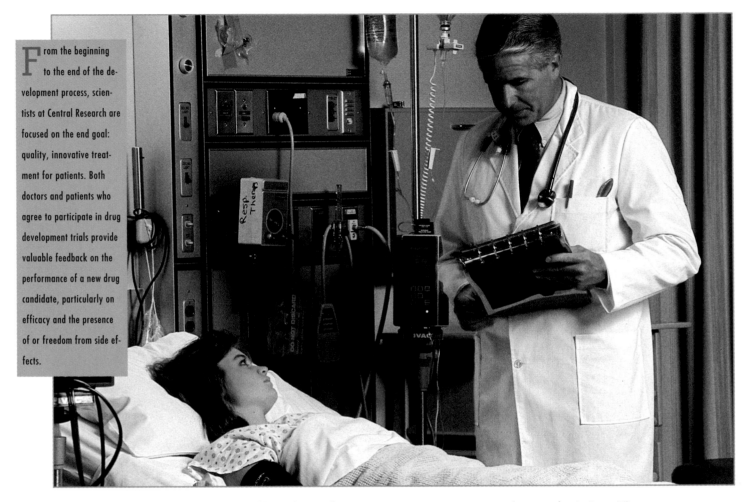

From the beginning to the end of the development process, scientists at Central Research are focused on the end goal: quality, innovative treatment for patients. Both doctors and patients who agree to participate in drug development trials provide valuable feedback on the performance of a new drug candidate, particularly on efficacy and the presence of or freedom from side effects.

"This kind of work calls for a different kind of person than late-stage research needs," continues Saxton. "You need scientist-physicians, preferably with clinical and laboratory research experience. They form the bridge between the discovery operations that generate the new drugs and the clinical operations that develop the clinical programs through late Phase II and Phase III to support regulatory submission. They are not constrained by the same logistical complexities as their colleagues in later-stage development. They have much more freedom to operate. They can do creative and insightful clinical experiments with smaller numbers of patients, and they can acquire some pretty exciting data by applying the right technical tools."

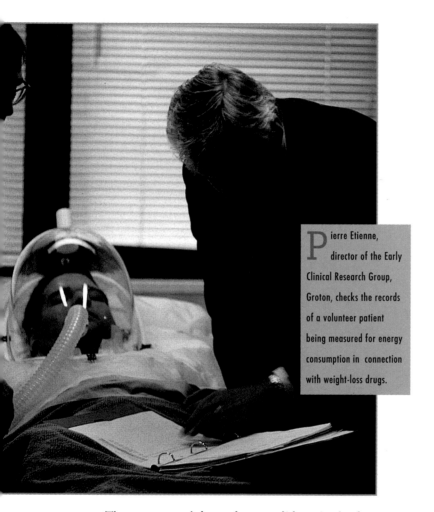

Pierre Etienne, director of the Early Clinical Research Group, Groton, checks the records of a volunteer patient being measured for energy consumption in connection with weight-loss drugs.

There are several dozen drug candidates in the development portfolio of the Early Clinical Research Group. Members of the ECRG work closely with Discovery, designing the early studies that are going to take place in man. ECRG is now about 40 strong at Groton, under the direction of Group Director Pierre Etienne, and almost as large at Sandwich, where it is directed by Garth Rapeport.

"In exploratory development, we try to make decisions as soon as possible about whether a drug should go into full Phase III," says Jeff Stritar, M.D., executive director of the Department of Clinical Research. "We cannot afford to follow thousands of patients for several years to see if a drug has an effect. We need to make decisions more quickly, to determine if a drug has real potential, to give us the encouragement to invest what is necessary to prove it."

The first thing ECRG does is study healthy volunteers to assure that the drug is absorbed when taken orally and to ascertain how long it lasts in the body. ECRG also determines whether or not there are any gross safety problems limiting the doses that can be used.

Whenever possible, the group tries to use a "surrogate marker" as an indicator of efficacy, something that can be measured quickly and efficiently to help make decisions on whether to go ahead or not. With antibiotics, the surrogate marker is simple – have sufficient levels of drug been achieved in the blood or tissues of patients to be comparable to concentrations of the antibiotic that kill bacteria in a test tube.

With other drugs, finding a surrogate marker requires a lot more ingenuity. In developing a drug for obesity, the end point is weight loss. Rather than follow hundreds of patients for a year or so to see if a new drug these earliest efforts as more focused on the potential of the unknown for generating excitement and smells, rather than on any systematic study.

George Milne's serious academic study of chemistry began at Yale under the tutelage of Professor William von Eggers Doering. After receiving his BSC degree in 1965 and with the support of his wife Carol, a Duke graduate, he continued his studies at MIT with Professor George Büchie. He was

nal chemistry section of central nervous system drugs, working with Chuck Harbert and later joining John Niblack on the chemical side of antivirals research, he changed careers in his fifth year. Following postdoctoral studies in pharmacology at the Medical College of Virginia, he joined Pfizer's Pharmacology Department in 1975 to undertake a new laboratory career in biological research on the central nervous system. This led to pioneering work and publication on

George M. Milne, Jr.

George Milne was born in New York, spent his earliest days in the farming community of Gilead, Connecticut, and started his education in a two room school in Scotland.

He remembers always being curious and having broad interests. "Growing up I was an enthusiastic, albeit undiscriminating, collector (birds' nests, stamps, rocks), a designer and builder of huts, woodsman (with father and grandfather) and amateur experimentalist."

Milne's interest in chemistry started at age 12 under the tutelage of an inspired science teacher. That year he received a Gilbert Chemistry set which he set up on a bench in the basement next to his birds' nests and other collections. He recalls

awarded his Ph.D. in 1969 for his work on the biosynthesis of aflatoxins, a family of powerful fungal carcinogens. He completed his professional training in chemistry as an NIH Post-doctoral Fellow with Eugene Van Tamelem at Stanford University.

Milne joined Pfizer in 1970, as the last chemist to be recruited directly by Barry Bloom from his old alma mater (MIT). "I first met Bloom early one morning outside my lab. I thought he was lost and asked if I could help him find his way. He soon made it clear that he knew his way well, and in the end, he was the key to my finding my way to Pfizer instead of the faculty at the University of Chicago."

George Milne's career at Pfizer is unusual in its diversity. Starting in the medici-

the cannabinoids, the active constituents of marijuana. While he was manager, and ultimately director, of CNS and Infectious Diseases, Zoloft, Unasyn, Zithromax and tenidap were developed.

In 1985, in a third change of direction, he became vice president of Research and Development Operations with responsibility for building Pfizer's first portfolio of external biotechnology investments. In 1996 this portfolio encompasses over 20 significant collaborations and investments with an annual budget of more than $80 million. Building further on his business experience, Milne served as the founding chairman of Pfizer's Pharmaceutical Steering Committee in 1993.

George Milne continued to pursue broad interests outside of his professional career as chair of the New York Botanical Gardens' International Committee for Systemic Botany, as a board member of Summer Music, the executive Committee of the Board of Trustees of Connecticut College and the International Society for Infectious Diseases. Through his membership in the Explorer's Club, he has participated in two working expeditions to the Amazonian Rain Forest and more recently the Arctic.

Milne was named president of Pfizer Central Research in 1993 at a critical time of challenge to the pharmaceutical industry. He is determined to see Pfizer achieve a sustained place as the leading innovator to meet the health-care needs of the people of the world.

George Milne, current president of Pfizer Central Research, has led the company's effort to stay on the cutting edge of pharmaceuticals research by exploring the various fields of biotechnology. He has had the opportunity to make his vision for Central Research a reality with a number of important investments in biotechnology that promise to maintain Pfizer's position as a leading innovator.

leads to a sufficient loss of weight, Pfizer researchers have used caloric expenditure as a surrogate. They measured how many calories were expanded during ordinary activity when a patient was using the candidate drug compared to a patient who was not using it. When the patients on medication expended a larger number of calories, the researchers took this as an indication that, if sustained, the drug would lead to weight loss over a longer period. With drugs affecting the central nervous system, one surrogate used is an imaging technique called positron emission tomography which indicates the ability of a drug candidate to bind to specific receptors in the brain.

For the potential treatment of Alzheimer's, drugs called anti-cholinesterase inhibitors slow the degradation of a neurotransmitter called acetylcholine, making the pathways in the brain that use this neurotransmitter more active – pathways that are known to be involved in memory and other cognitive functions. Rather than initially studying a hundred or more Alzheimer's patients for six months, the researchers used the effects of scopolamine, a drug marketed for motion sickness, as a surrogate. Scopolamine blocks the effects of acetylcholine and, as a consequence, has undesirable side effects that are similar to the symptoms of Alzheimer's disease – inability to concentrate and memory problems, which can be measured in simple recall tests involving a series of numbers. When

given scopolamine, a volunteer can only repeat a few of the numbers. When given scopolamine and a candidate drug, he can do much better; the drug reverses the effects of scopolamine with this surrogate efficacy signal allowing a dose range for efficiency to be defined. Pfizer has gone on to find similar effects with Alzheimer's patients and has taken such a drug into Phase II development.

In developing a drug for irritable bowel syndrome (IBS), a surrogate marker measurement technique developed in Sandwich was based on a computerized integrated signal measuring the amplitude and frequency of pressure changes in the large intestine. Using this internally developed technology, the Early Clinical Research Group tested a drug candidate to see if it had the desired effect of reducing the size and amount of pressure waves in the intestine. A similar idea has been used to evaluate drugs for urinary incontinence. By placing a pressure-sensing device in the bladder and filling the bladder with saline solution, researchers were able to measure how much solution could be introduced before a pressure wave occurred and the bladder expelled. They then administered the candidate drug, observing that not only could they get a larger amount of solution into the bladder before the pressure wave occurred, but also the pressure wave was much smaller. The pressure served as a surrogate for the true clinical end point, which is being able to go longer without having to void.

The Early Clinical Research Groups have bridged the gap between the laboratory scientist and the heavy investment phase of full clinical development. By rapidly exploring new drug candidates in innovative early clinical experiments, they are making pharmaceutical research more efficient.

Phase III Clinical Trials

In contrast to the experimental and evolving process of early trials and tests, Phase III – on which hinges the possibility of regulatory approval and commercial success – is a heavily regulated, tremendously expensive undertaking, involving clinical trials with thousands of patients at a cost of several tens of millions of dollars. Before embarking on this path, Pfizer must ask itself some crucial questions: Is it worth the investment? Does the drug candidate have the necessary points of differentiation from other, competing drugs? Is it something that doctors will want to prescribe? That patients will want to be treated with? That third-party payers will want to pay for? Is it so clear an improvement over existing therapy that patient advocacy groups and professional organizations will demand it be made readily available?

Before entering Phase III, there has to be proof that the drug is tolerated well, has no safety concerns and has a reasonable chance of being effective in a defined dosage range for the disease it was designed to treat. Because it would be too expensive to investigate five or six doses, researchers try to narrow the dose range to two or three – say, 5, 10 and 20 milligrams – which are in the neighborhood surrounding the dose projected as the most promising.

Given a go-ahead by the corporate level committee known as the Development Planning Committee (DPC), Phase III can begin; it may involve 50 to 100 individual study sites containing the target patients and located, for geographic diversity, throughout the world. These clinical sites are in many countries, including the United States, Canada, Mexico, Central and South America, Europe, Japan, Australia and Africa. (Clinical research will soon be done in China and India, as well).

Says Steven Ryder, vice president of Clinical Development: "Because we want to obtain registration in all these places, we do local research – with local experts – to help them make a benefit-risk judgment leading to approval. Medical therapy and societal standards vary dramatically throughout the world. It is entirely possible for regulators from different countries to examine the same set of data on a drug and to come to different conclusions. The Japanese, for example, have very low thresholds of tolerance for side effects as compared with Western societies, and they require their own extensive clinical trials."

Testing drugs in clinical trials in the United States is the job of Dilip Mehta, M.D., senior vice president for Clinical Research, and in Europe, David McGibney, vice president for Clinical Research. Each year, the department receives about 350,000 to 400,000 pages of patient data from the United States and almost as much from Europe. Each page has 20 to 50 different items on it, from the patient's name, age and sex to his or her blood pressure and other clinical measurements. To handle the data alone requires the labors of some 250 people, about 150 in Groton and 100 in Sandwich, Pfizer's headquarters for European Clinical Research (Euroclin). Out of this mass of information the idea of a computerized system called PfizerClin was born.

When William Accomando, executive director of Biostatistics and Clinical Systems, was assigned to tackle the problem in 1987, Sandwich and Groton were using different computerized data-handling systems, CRESS in Sandwich and Clintrial in Groton. When it came time to combine data for submission to regulatory agencies, it was a very difficult, time-consuming affair.

After interviewing people in both places – clinicians, clinical research associates, statisticians – Accomando's department, in conjunction with the counterpart in Sandwich, developed a prototype to demonstrate what a new single system called PfizerClin could do. Finally, in 1991, they started putting data on Pfizer's drugs into the system, and ultimately PfizerClin was adopted and will be used companywide.

Data is entered into PfizerClin from case report forms made out by physicians. The system also allows for electronic data capture from outside laboratories that send Pfizer test results directly off computers that the company has given to about 200 physicians. PfizerClin automatically calls each doctor's computer in the evening, retrieves the data from it and loads it into the database.

To verify that the data is correct, edit checks are run regularly. These ensure, for instance, that a male is not inadvertently listed in a study of hysterectomies. Any errors are printed out and given to a clinical research associate, who contacts the investigating physician and finds out how to correct them. PfizerClin also allows the company to transfer data electronically to the FDA. At present, a larger more comprehensive computer system for global clinical data storage, called HERMES, is being rolled out.

Since Dilip Mehta joined Clinical Research in 1982, his department has experienced dramatic growth, most of it in the last four or five years. At the time of Mehta's arrival, the whole department consisted of 55 or

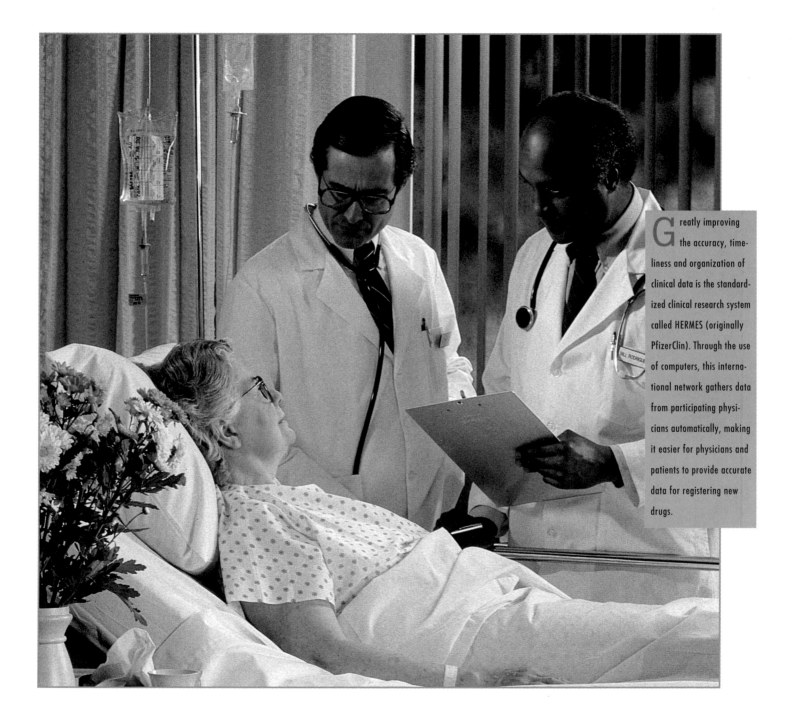

G reatly improving the accuracy, timeliness and organization of clinical data is the standardized clinical research system called HERMES (originally PfizerClin). Through the use of computers, this international network gathers data from participating physicians automatically, making it easier for physicians and patients to provide accurate data for registering new drugs.

a drug will not have an adverse effect. We have to ask a patient, how many days off from work did you have to take, how good do you feel, what's the impact on your sex life? All this data is putting a tremendous burden on our information-processing systems. When one looks at the NDAs we submitted in the 1980s versus the NDA we recently submitted for tenidap, there is a staggering difference in size, and the next NDA will be even larger."

An even harder part of outcomes research is assessing the potential economic impact of a drug on society. If an Alzheimer's patient can be made to sleep through the night so that his caregiver can get a good night's rest, what's that worth in terms of an improvement in the quality of life? If a drug can treat panic disorder, the inability to interact with human beings without panicking, the person treated can get on with his career. What's that worth?

Outcomes Research

Information that is gathered on patients who receive a candidate drug, a placebo or a traditional agent is the basis for the demonstration that a drug is effective and safe. Data-gathering is getting more complicated: the number of patients is Increasing, the duration of studies is increasing and the amount of information that is gathered at each patient visit is increasing. Researchers are handling more data because the state of the art of medicine has improved and regulators are constantly increasing requirements.

"We measure more things, says Steven Ryder, vice president of Clinical Development. "We now have different subtypes of cholesterol, for example. We have more parameters we have to follow to show that

While the clinical trials are going forward, an important part of the worldwide effort is what is called "outcomes research," which tries to measure the impact of drug therapy on the state of a person's life, the impact on the payer and the impact on society. One objective is to predict the economic consequences of therapy using the drug in question, beyond the cost of the drug itself. "What is relevant is the *total* cost for the treatment of the patient's illness," says Ryder. "If the pharmacy pays two dollars less for a drug but the patient comes back for surgery, the payer is going to lose money. Unfortunately, not all payers see it that way; they simply demand that the initial cost of the drug be lower."

Pfizer, for example, is developing drugs that will be uniquely effective in the treatment of both depression and anxiety. Many people display symptoms that are hard to pin down to either depression or anxiety, so a doctor doesn't know whether to prescribe an antidepresssant or an anxiolytic. Pfizer's agents will simplify the doctor's life, and that of a managed-care organization, in that there will be fewer patients who come back because of the wrong therapy being administered. Pfizer thinks it can show that such a drug will have a tangible economic benefit.

"Outcomes research is complex and evolving," says Ryder. "It requires improvements in our ability to capture the right information and probably experts to help us with the interpretation of the data because it doesn't always give us clear answers. Politicians, who are going to be making our regulations, often make these simplistic statements that all you have to do is mandate that drug companies put up money to do a comparison between Drug A and Drug B, and then you simply make the choice. It's not as simple as that."

"The environment will be less forgiving in the future," Ryder concludes. "We are trying many different things; almost every program is an experiment both in terms of the drug and the ways that we test it. The necessity to constantly improve is going to become more and more demanding. It's going to be a much tougher business. We at Pfizer are in better shape than some companies, but it still is going to be a rocky road."

60 people; today there are about 450 in Groton alone. The number of medical doctors has increased from 7 or 8 to 40; the number of Ph.D.s, from 5 or 6 to 30 or 40. Expenditures for testing patients have grown from $5 million a year to $40 million or more. Clinical Research used to generate 60,000 pages of data annually; now the figure is up to 600,000 pages. Today about 1,000 doctors around the United States are testing Pfizer's new drugs on some 6,000 to 8,000 patients a year.

Although recent innovations in nearly every phase of development are helping to smooth out a traditionally complicated process, the area of clinical development still has great potential for modernization. While John Niblack is sanguine, he sees clinical development as a major focus in the future. "In contrast to the biotech revolution, the science of clinical testing has progressed little since the 1950s. We have the opportunity to discover all these exciting new medicines, but our tools for measuring their effects in various disease processes have fallen far behind.

"In the area of rheumatoid arthritis, for example, we still evaluate a new drug by asking someone how stiff they felt when they got up in the morning and measure their swollen joints by fitting calibrated rings on their fingers. Although rheumatoid arthritis is perceived to be a chronic auto-immune state, scientists have still not

devised biochemical or immunological tests that can be performed on blood or body tissues to correlate with a patient's present and prognostic state. In Alzheimer's disease, all we have, basically, is a set of questionnaires to evaluate the patient. In depression, it's the same thing; we have rating scales that were worked out over 30 years ago. This is what we're working with – old, blunt tools – to measure the effects of new drugs. Until the revolu-

Just as technology has enabled scientists to speed drug screening processes and enhance drug targeting, advances in the procedures and tools of clinical trials will enable scientists to determine if all their effort has produced the desired effect on the patient. This modernization of clinical evaluations is one of Central Research's foremost goals for the future.

tion occurs on the clinical side, it's going to be slow going. Devising new tools, new clinical evaluation paradigms, is going to be the challenge of this decade and into the next century."

Clinical and Scientific Affairs

Conducting clinical trials to obtain additional indications and new dosage forms for drugs already approved is predominantly the job of Clinical and Scientific

Affairs (C&SA), a Central Research department of over 150 people located in Pfizer's New York headquarters.

In 1977, the Department of Clinical and Scientific Affairs was formed from the merger of two U.S. Pharmaceutical departments at the New York headquarters: Scientific Affairs and New Drug Development. The Department of Scientific Affairs had been a submissions group responsible for the preparation of NDAs for new indications and formulations of marketed drugs, licensed drugs and OTC drugs for the Consumer Healthcare Division. The Department of New Drug Development had been created in 1975 to conduct clinical trials for licensed and marketed drugs, which involved monitoring, statistical analysis and data processing, and compiling the medical sections of NDAs. At the time of the merger, the total staff of the Department of Clinical and Scientific Affairs consisted of 15 people.

The mission of the merged department was to achieve timely submission and rapid approval of NDAs for licensed drugs and new indications or formulations. This goal was achieved in the cases of the licensed drugs bacampicillin (Spectrobid), cefoperazone (Cefobid) and nifedipine (Procardia) where, in addition to the clinical work, all of the preclinical work was the responsibility of the department. Glipizide (Glucotrol) and cetirizine (Zyrtec) were also licensed drugs developed by C&SA.

In the early 1980s the GITS (gastrointestinal transit system) technology for a controlled-release dosage form was licensed from the Alza Corporation and used to develop greatly improved formulations for already successful Pfizer drugs. Thus, Procardia XL became Pfizer's first billion-dollar drug in the U.S. market, and Glucotrol XL had sales of 100 million dollars in its first year on the market. In the area of new indications, the department has been in-

volved in the development of Cardura for benign prostatic hyperplasia and Zoloft for obsessive compulsive disorder, panic disorder and post-traumatic stress disorder.

In 1992, the department, headed by Karen Scappaticci, executive director, was incorporated into Central Research and continued to operate out of New York headquarters. The department's efforts are now centrally managed and aligned with overall Central Research goals. In addition to working primarily on ex-

A pilot plant, such as the one pictured at left, serves the dual purpose of providing small and mid-sized batches of the drug to use in clinical testing as well as testing and refining the manufacturing process for a new drug. The pilot plant allows all the variables to be tested before the major investment for manufacturing a new drug is made.

tended development for new and approved drugs, the department is heavily involved in the defense of challenges to marketed products and has recently become involved with Rx-to-OTC switches

Developmental Research

New applications for existing products and licensing of outside candidates are two ways of keeping the development phase of the pipeline full. In addition, efficient use of its own resources is a critical way in which Pfizer is learning to increase the number of successful drug candidates. "Our prime objective in the next few years is to accelerate the progress of candidates that are further back in our pipeline into full development," concludes Saxton. "The output of Discovery has provided us with a rich portfolio. However, the high attrition rate in the early stages dictates that we identify potential winners as quickly and efficiently as possible to justify the huge costs of bringing them to the marketplace. Our Developmental Research organization is a critical contributor to this stage and to all stages of candidate progression."

Developmental Research was originally formed in 1969 under the leadership of Ken Chapman and later headed by Jim Tretter. It combined Process R&D, Analytical Research and Pharmaceutical R&D; it was the first time those three functions had been merged anywhere in the pharmaceutical industry. Developmental Research was established because Gerry Laubach, then head of Research, saw that a lack of sufficient clinical supplies was adversely affecting the rate of development of new products. With the addition of Bioprocess R&D in 1992, the Developmental Research Group now has about 700 people, 450 in the United States and 250 in Europe under George Mooney, group executive director, all tasked with synthesizing, purifying and analyzing drug candidates and then preparing suitable dosage forms for administration to animals and humans.

Says Dan O'Shea, presently senior vice president, Developmental Research, "When I joined Pfizer in

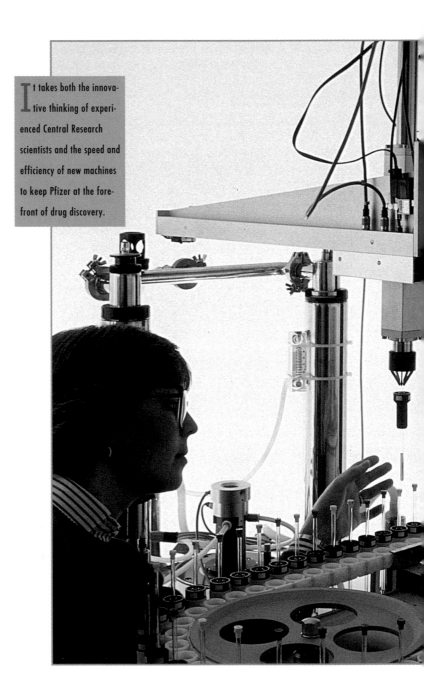

It takes both the innovative thinking of experienced Central Research scientists and the speed and efficiency of new machines to keep Pfizer at the forefront of drug discovery.

1969, we had a small pilot plant with four chemical reactors with a capacity of 400 gallons. Now we have access to vessels totaling 14,000 gallons. We are preparing huge amounts of bulk drug because safety studies require that we use much higher doses and because our clinical programs are much larger. We made three tons of bulk material for testing tenidap alone. What's exciting about Developmental Research is that we apply our expertise, in some cases unique expertise, over the 20 to 30-year lifetime of a successful drug, from the very early stages of discovery through its proof of clinical efficacy, regulatory filings, launch into the market and commercial support; ultimately we try to breed in proprietary improvements for our products so that they remain viable beyond their normal patent life. What I find particularly intriguing is that even though the time frames for drug development are so long and the attrition rates so high, at each particular stage, for each particular task, there's an enormous sense of urgency, and that urgency breeds extraordinary teamwork and excitement."

One particularly provocative example of that teamwork under time pressure goes back to 1973 and the development of an antibiotic called the penem tetrazole, coded CP-35,587. This was a particularly complex agent which required 21 separate synthetic steps, in-

volved unconventional, hazardous reagents like phosgene and sodium azide, and involved chemical intermediates that were all extremely unstable. In early October of 1973 a large synthesis team was assembled that at that time was unprecedented. The team included most of a Discovery Chemistry team, most of a Chemical Process Research Group under the leadership of Irv Goldman and 65 people from the Process R&D Department. In total, there were some 20 laboratories and over 100 synthesis-oriented personnel trying to make 2.5 kg of CP-35,587 to meet the "Thanksgiving toxicology slot." Since so little was known about the downstream chemistry and so much process improvement would be required to meet the goal, supplying the process research labs with substrate from their experimentation was a critical and ever-present challenge. Through an enormous effort, which required three shifts and 80-100 hours per week from many workers, the "Thanksgiving slot" was achieved, ultimately supporting clinical testing in the first quarter of 1974.

Beyond the enormity of the task, the speed with which it was accomplished and the extraordinary logistical challenges that were met, the most impressive lasting aspect was the team camaraderie and spirit. The team's motivation came from the feeling that they were playing an important role in attempting to bring an im-

Since the creation of Central Research, Pfizer's pilot production facilities have nearly quadrupled, matching the demand for clinical supplies of drugs in Pfizer's full pipeline. The U.S. Pharmaceutical Group's Groton pilot plant manufactures test quantities of a drug in development by carefully monitoring conditions with a network of computers, right.

portant new therapeutic advance to infectious disease therapy. Unfortunately, after the first clinical experiments, it was quickly discovered that CP-35,587 was too rapidly cleared from the systemic circulation and its viability as a new anti-infective agent was seriously flawed. Subsequently, Discovery scientists identified several other candidates, all of which had the same type of synthesis challenge. These compounds were also prepared in a timely way, but in the end, they all suffered from this rapid clearance in humans.

"There are retirees today who still get excited about their contribution to this enormous penem tetrazole project, even though all that energy, all that investment and all that excitement did not lead to a successful drug candidate," says O'Shea. "In Developmental Research we always have a number of candidates in development in which we invest our heart and soul, knowing that most will not lead to successful products. On the other hand, all successful products, at one time or another, come through Developmental Research, and we

The manufacture of a drug candidate takes place in facilities very similar to full-scale manufacturing facilities, left. The size of the reactor tanks and the quantity produced are the primary difference between pilot plants and a typical manufacturing facility.

Animal tests were pretty simple at the time, and were done primarily at Maywood, New Jersey. Following the Kefauver amendments of 1962, both the thinking of the industry and the requirements of the FDA became more extensive, and more animals were treated for longer periods of time, including lifetime studies of animals for possible carcinogenic effects. Pfizer complied with those requirements, expanding the department under Charles Delahunt as director of Toxicology.

advantage. They are linked by a computer system that enables them to share data just as easily as if the studies had been conducted next door.

"Toxicology research is a lot more complex than it used to be, much more regulated," observes Schach von Wittenau. "Thirty years ago you used a few animals for testing before going into man, and the decisions on whether the animal data were adequate or not were made primarily by the clinicians here and at the FDA. Now the

The Development of Toxicology

Drug Safety Evaluation, a group of some 240 people formerly headed by Manfred Schach von Wittenau, senior vice president, is responsible for conducting safety evaluations of new drug candidates and also for the care and handling of all the animals used in testing new drugs.

When Schach von Wittenau, known as "von Schach" by his colleagues, came to Pfizer as a chemist from MIT in 1958, he worked in the tetracycline area for five or six years before becoming head of a small drug metabolism group started by Rex Pinson, then assistant director of Pharmacology, which was assigned to examine what happened to drugs after they were absorbed in the bodies of animals.

"At the time, toxicology didn't have many scientifically sophisticated practitioners," Rex Pinson recalls. "The tendency was to do the testing by rote. But gradually we developed experiments that gave a better idea of why things were happening, so that a better judgment of the relevance of the animal findings to human safety could be deduced."

In 1973, Schach von Wittenau was made responsible for the Toxicology Department, now known as Drug Safety Evaluation. In the 1980s he launched a new era of cooperation among the Toxicology units at Groton, Amboise and Nagoya. Today these three groups jointly develop the packages for worldwide registration of new Pfizer drugs, utilizing each other's resources to the best

whole process is very formalized. The regulators supply us with elaborate checklists to follow. We have to conduct studies according to so-called Good Laboratory Practices (GLP), which means that all the data have to be verified by an auditor, and signatures have to be attached to everything.

"As a result of the increase in attention paid to bureaucratic detail, our capacity for testing has gone down about 30 percent. Now we have a ratio of almost one staff auditor to one staff toxicologist."

One hopeful note has been struck by the International Conference on Harmonization, which was started in the late 1980s in the context of the European Economic Community. Prior to the conference, all 12 countries in the EEC had different regulations for the testing and evaluation of drugs, but at the first major meeting, held in 1991 in Brussels, progress was made on "harmonization" of the varying requirements, not only in Europe but also in the United States and Japan. Pfizer, like other pharmaceutical companies, is vitally concerned with the eventual outcome of these discussions, which could eliminate the repetitive testing now required in various countries in addition to that already done in the United States, thus saving animals, time and expenses.

Schach von Wittenau retired from Pfizer in 1995; Drug Safety Evaluation is now directed by Guy Paulus.

do get to celebrate their market successes." The tradition that was evident in the penem tetrazole effort is still in evidence today: that can-do attitude, the excitement about improving processes, creating new drug systems and analytical methodologies and most importantly, of playing a useful role in trying to improve health care through a team effort.

For the Zolofts and Zithromaxes that do make it to the marketplace, the next element of the challenge for Developmental Research is to transfer the technology into the commercial arena. While smooth technology transfer has always been a hallmark at Pfizer, a variety of factors have dictated transfer to commercial scale *prior* to Phase III, thereby necessitating the acceleration of technology development by several years. Buzz Cue, senior executive director of Developmental Research says that "the time to identify and refine the optimum chemistry has been cut by 33-50 percent, while at the same time, the need for more information concerning environmental and worker-safety issues has increased exponentially. But in true Pfizer tradition, in conjunction with our manufacturing and Quality Control colleagues in USPG and IPG, we're creating new ways to meet this challenge." Exemplifying this interdivisional partnership, in June of 1995, a new, fully automated synthesis facility opened in Groton with one-sixth of the reactors dedicated to Cen-

tral Research needs. "Not only will this large facility satisfy the increasing demand for developmental supplies, it serves as the first stage in technology transfer and provokes user-friendly synthesis," says Cue.

Tim Hagen, group director of Pharmaceutical R&D points out: "Starting in 1993, Central Research demands on the Brooklyn dosage-form manufacturing has grown to the point where two full teams with members from Pharmaceutical R&D, Analytical, Manufacturing and Quality Control are on site in Brooklyn at all times. Our worldwide Phase III suppliers for both Sandwich and Groton candidates are now prepared in Brooklyn, and technology transfer is basically completed coincident with Phase III." Comparable relationships also exist between Central Research scientists and International/Pharmaceutical Synthesis Groups in Ireland, France and Germany.

Developmental Research also collaborates with medical and marketing teams to create new dosage forms and delivery systems to expand the utility of products. Helen Hangac, manager of Analytical R&D, who was the azithromycin analytical chemist and has followed the "evergreening" of Zithromax, says, "We initially registered and launched the capsule form. Illustrating the fertile opportunities for dosage form elaboration, we have now developed a powder for oral suspension for pediatrics and a sachet to be mixed with the child's favorite liquid, as well as a chewable tablet. While Zithromax may be particularly rich in new dosage form opportunities, all advanced products have about two or three evergreening concepts under development."

In 1992 the Bioprocess R&D Department, formerly in the Chemicals R&D Group, joined Developmental Research, and they are incorporating their tradition of fermentation expertise into pharmaceutical research. "A living microorganism can efficiently construct molecules that are too large or too complex to be made economically by chemical synthesis alone. For example, the area of infectious diseases is an excellent opportunity for fermentation and always has been," says Ken Taksen, executive director of Bioprocess R&D. "Most of the major antibiotics have been fermentation-derived or chemically synthesized from a fermentation building block. And there are certainly opportunities in related animal health areas for anti-infectives, for antiparasitics and for growth promotants. We are also doing some work in finding immunosuppressants to combat rejection of organ transplants. Another great opportunity may be in plant extracts, using fermentation technology to produce medicines more cheaply than you could by growing the plants themselves."

Bioprocess R&D has been fully integrated into the medicinal research efforts and is playing an important role in providing natural product substrate to the discovery efforts, both for human and animal health, and has demonstrated the flexibility of broadly applying this special expertise. For example, a gene therapy team was just commissioned, serving as another sign of that can-do attitude and Pfizer's flexibility to apply expertise where it's needed.

7

CHAPTER SEVEN

Animal Health and Food Science

In Australia, a worker tends a chute handling cattle that will be used in experiments with drugs for animal health. Right, Terramycin is incorporated into various feed supplements to prevent worms in livestock.

Animal Health

Pfizer's success in developing drugs to promote human health has been paralleled by its triumphs in the fields of animal health and food-related products.

The company's early animal health accomplishments owed much to a major drug developed for human use – Terramycin. Its use as a feed supplement for animals got off to a colorful start. Shortly after Pfizer's Agricultural Division was launched in the early 1950s, someone had the brilliant idea of promoting APF Plus, a Terramycin-based feed supplement for animals, with a grand hog-judging contest at Chicago's Conrad Hilton Hotel. The affair, crowed Jerry Thompson, Ag's new manager, "had newsreel men hanging on the chandeliers."

Hanging from the chandeliers might have been a good idea when a couple of the pigs got loose and began running through the hotel's lobby. "There was quite a bedlam," recalls Bob Wornick, who was in charge of the event. "Those two-hundred-pound rascals can run like the devil. All these guys yelling, 'hoo, hoo, hoo,' trying to get them back in their cages. One of the hogs got into an elevator and the poor girl who was running it went shrieking out of the car when this monster came charging in." The *Chicago Tribune* headlined the story "Pigs Loose at the Hilton."

Undismayed – perhaps encouraged by the publicity – Ag decided to bring a steer to a press conference at the Waldorf-Astoria Hotel in New York.

"They found a pretty good-looking steer, got him into a truck and unloaded him in front of the Waldorf," says Wornick, who had the duty once more. "Of course, the first problem is that you cannot get a steer through a revolving door, and the side doors were too narrow. No one had thought about that detail. So there we were, all outside on the sidewalk with a 1,200-pound steer. We got the engineers out of the Waldorf to remove the revolving door. Meanwhile, we were trying to keep this poor animal quiet because he wasn't used to traffic and crowds."

When the steer finally got in, the manager seemed to be on the verge of a heart attack, and two boys from the hotel's staff rushed about with little brooms and polished brass scoops, ineffectively trying to remedy the nervous animal's ultimate reaction. The upshot was that an entire section of carpeting had to be taken up for cleaning.

Otherwise, the proceedings were deemed a great success. The press got its pictures. A waiter in a white jacket came in with a silver tray with a cover that he lifted to reveal a neat little pile of hay, which he offered to the steer.

With such illustrious events, Pfizer entered the animal health business.

To be more precise, the company got into the business by putting Terramycin in a variety of animal products – hog feed, chicken feed, cow feed – under a multitude of labels, from TM-5 to Terralac. Terramycin, it seems, enabled animals to utilize their feed more efficiently, make larger weight gains and maintain better health on less feed.

A 700-acre Agricultural Research and Development Center was established in 1952 at Terre Haute, Indiana, where the company already had a fermentation plant for the manufacture of streptomycin, and where it began large-scale production of Terramycin. Using an old government hospital on the grounds, Pfizer U.S. Animal Health built offices and laboratories with the aim of studying animal health and nutrition. A veterinary section was started to study livestock and poultry diseases.

By the late 1970s, Pfizer had developed an injectable, long-acting form of Terramycin called Terramycin/LA for international markets. At Lee's Summit, Missouri, Joyce Davis, above, tests the product in the quality control laboratory as scientists handle the final product, right. From left are: Mark Pinkston, Jay Rash, Jim Muren and Cal Downing. Terramycin "Scours" tablets treat bacterial enteritis and pneumonia in calves.

In 1959, following the passage of the "Delaney Amendment," Al Greene, then the corporate officer responsible for Research, shut down the facility. In 1963, it was reopened under the direction of Groton Research. In the late 1960s, the reorganization and research finally paid off when several pioneering projects resulted in the introduction of a number of highly successful drugs.

The first of these was Mecadox (carbadox), which treated bacterial infections (especially swine dysentery) in young pigs and promoted faster growth. This product, discovered by Lloyd Conover's Chemotherapy Research Group in Groton, was so successful that it became the market leader in many parts of the world and fostered widespread counterfeiting overseas. It is still on the market and registering growth each year.

Among the highlights of drug discovery in this era were the anthelmintics pyrantel (Strongid, Banminth) and morantel (Rumatel, Paratect). The former found application in pigs, horses and dogs, the latter in cattle and sheep. New modes of drug use came out of this project as well. For example, superior disease control was achieved using pyrantel prophylactically in the feed of young pigs. Traditionally, adult animals were treated

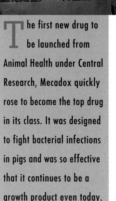

The first new drug to be launched from Animal Health under Central Research, Mecadox quickly rose to become the top drug in its class. It was designed to fight bacterial infections in pigs and was so effective that it continues to be a growth product even today.

only after worm parasites had already caused disease.

Also initiated in the testing of this product was the combination of two independently acting drugs into a single dosing formula. The combination of Banminth and Mecadox became the largest selling feed additive for pigs in the U.S. In the early years of this additive's marketing (mid-1970s), Agricultural Products R&D mounted a "high tech" market-support effort designed to demonstrate the unique economic and disease control benefits of the "Banminth/Mecadox Program" to farmers reluctant to adopt new ways. This program, conceived by Curt Askelson and led by Bob Ranier, focused on involving non-Pfizer scientific and marketing opinion leaders in an intensive effort to show the superiority of these products. It hailed a major new departure in the marketing of animal health products in the U.S.

Out of the Banminth research came another product called Strongid (pyrantel pamoate), which is more slowly absorbed, has a slower build-up in tissues and hence is suitable for more sensitive animals like pigs, horses, pets and even humans (under the trade names of Combantrin and Antiminth). In fact, pyrantel pamoate was the only Pfizer animal health drug that developed an application for humans as well.

One of the earliest collaborations between Sandwich and Groton, research on this antihelmintic, led by Bill Austin in Sandwich and Lloyd Conover in Groton, created some controversy on both sides. To some extent, the Sandwich and Groton research teams viewed each other as competitors. To the credit of Conover and Austin, the project eventually met with success when morantel and pyrantel were patented by Pfizer.

The inventors, listed as Lloyd Conover, Bill Austin and Jim McFarland, along with the parasitologists from both continents – Rendle Cornwell and Mervyn Jones from Sandwich, John Lynch and Harold Howes from Groton and Vasillios Theodoides from Terre Haute – had paved the way for future collaborations in the Animal Health and Agricultural Divisions. In addition to the collaborative aspect of the invention of morantel and pyrantel, the medicinal chemistry research for this project was the first instance of extensive use of the Hantsch Analysis, one of the earliest and most effective methods for guiding rational drug design.

When Lloyd Conover took over the Agricultural Products R&D Division in 1975, he was given orders

The anthelmintic Banminth (pyrantel) was perfected to rid pigs, horses and dogs of worms and is used in the feed of young pigs to prevent worms. In the mid-1970s, in a revolution in the marketing of animal health products, Banminth was combined with Mecadox to become the largest-selling feed additive for pigs in the U.S.

that his first priority should be supporting, defending or improving products already on the market. The U.S. Ag Division was doing poorly, and there were recurring rumors that Pfizer was considering selling it. "I took the Ag job with some misgivings," says Conover, "because animal health research had always been a poor relation in what was basically a human-drug research organization. Budgets had been held essentially at a no-growth level for several years. I sought reassurance that Pfizer was really committed to animal health R&D." He was told to help turn the business around with products already in hand or it would be lost. An enhanced discovery effort would have to wait.

On his first day in Groton as head of the new Agricultural Products R&D Division in January 1975, Conover was surprised to be asked by Barry Bloom to attend a presentation about Pfizer's recently acquired corn and soybean seed businesses. Soon thereafter, Gerry Laubach handed Conover the task of assessing the likely impact of gene manipulation techniques on commercial crop-plant breeding. After giving himself a crash course in genetics and plant breeding, Conover concluded that if Pfizer hoped to become a

A Pfizer researcher carefully examines sprouting soybeans in 1977. The company had acquired a soybean and corn seed business and scientists were soon assessing the impact of gene manipulation on crop-plant breeding. They were the first to transform corn by introducing foreign genes, giving it resistance to herbicides.

leader in the crop seed business, it would have to undertake laboratory research on plant genetics.

He then set out to find someone to build and run the program. He picked Tom Rice, then a research associate at Michigan State University working on plant tissue culture. The research team Rice created went on to become a world leader in the field. They were the first researchers to transform corn by introducing foreign genes. In their initial work, the altered genes gave corn herbicide resistance and passed on these traits to subsequent seed generations. Later, Pfizer entered into a joint venture with DeKalb, forming DeKalb-Pfizer Genetics, with Pfizer owning a minority interest. The joint research in pursuit of improved seeds lasted until 1990, when Pfizer sold its interest back to DeKalb.

In following the assigned mission of making the most of the animal health drugs, Pfizer had already developed two new products: Paratect bolus (containing morantel) and Terramycin/LA. Both could be clearly differentiated from the original products in terms of efficacy in the field.

Paratect bolus represented both a revolutionary mode of control of intestinal worms in grazing cattle and a novel prolonged-release delivery system. The disease-control concept, originated by parasitologists Rendle Cornwell and Mervyn Jones in Sandwich, was based upon

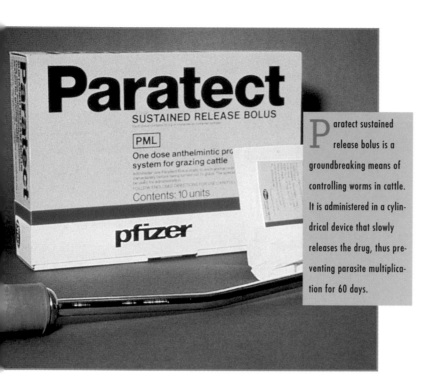

Paratect sustained release bolus is a groundbreaking means of controlling worms in cattle. It is administered in a cylindrical device that slowly releases the drug, thus preventing parasite multiplication for 60 days.

their knowledge of the annual parasite life cycle. Continuous release of drug in the first stomach (rumen) of calves for 60 days in the spring blocked the parasite "multiplication" stage, and this prevented the harmful heavy infection which naturally occurred in late summer. This project entailed an unprecedented level of interdepartmental and transatlantic collaboration.

The Paratect bolus consisted of a metal cylinder enclosed at each end by a drug-releasing membrane. The final design was perfected by Dave Dresback of Pharmaceutical R&D, working under Don Monkhouse and Armando Aguiar, while Alan Curtiss from the Diagnostics

Group designed the equipment for manufacturing the device. The field trials, designed and supervised by Mervyn Jones, were of unprecedented complexity. They had to be tailored to varying grazing practices and climate conditions in different parts of the world – and they involved treating animals when they showed no sign of disease.

The work on improving the drug delivery system continued and produced another new design featuring a drug-infused, perforated-sheet matrix which was administered in cylindrical form, then was held in the rumen as a flattened sheet.

Injectable Terramycin had been one of the mainstays of Pfizer's animal health business worldwide since the 1950s. By 1975, much of this business had been lost to generic products. Pfizer recognized that a long-acting (96-hour) injectable dosage form would have great commercial appeal because of labor-saving convenience and superior efficacy.

In 1975, the Agricultural Products R&D Division made this a top-priority project and by the late 1970s, had developed a long-acting, injectable form of Terramycin called Terramycin/LA in international markets and Liquamycin LA-200 in Canada and the United States. The drug was incorporated into a solution that wasn't absorbed immediately but was slowly released from the injection site over a period of three or four days, allowing farmers to give their cattle a single dose instead of repeated daily injections. The new delivery system provided activity over a longer period while maintaining acceptable muscle toleration and residue characteristics.

Terramycin/LA once again showcased the collaborative efforts of Groton, Terre Haute and Sandwich. Saurabhkuar Desai of Pharmaceutical R&D in Groton again came through with an innovative product, as Curt Askelson, Bill Babcock, Bob Ranier and Lawrence Davey worked on biological evaluation and field trials.

Since its development, Liquamycin/Terramycin/LA has found new applications and has become one of Pfizer's largest-selling animal health products. It is used in cattle, swine, horses and dogs, each with a slightly different formulation, and it is useful against pneumonia in calves and respiratory infections in pigs. In cases where many young animals are kept in close quarters, disease can spread like wildfire. Here, Terramycin/LA is used not only for treatment, but also to prevent a potential epidemic from spreading.

Fully aware of the difficulties of persuading farmers to trust their livelihood to new disease-control methods, Pfizer went to extensive lengths to educate farmers as to the benefits of these new delivery systems. Unfortunately, this marketing effort paid off for Pfizer's

Breach Farm, Pfizer's animal research facility is near the Sandwich research center. Started in 1970 at the suggestion of Clive Briggs, former head of Animal Health R&D in the U.K., the 300-acre spread has grown considerably. Here sheep and cattle are tested with drugs under actual farm conditions.

competitors as well. Merck's intrinsically long-acting parasiticide, Ivomec, met with significant consumer demand and spurred Pfizer to the challenge of producing a superior product. With demand and awareness on the rise, however, Pfizer was perfectly positioned to fulfill farmers' demand for innovative and powerful new drugs.

During Conover's tenure (1975-1984) at Agricultural Products R&D, major expansions and improve-

Pfizer's Animal Health products are field tested just as human drugs are. On a sheep ranch in Australia, a subject is injected with Terramycin in 1963 while a Pfizer Animal Health representative looks on.

ments of large animal-testing facilities were carried out both in the U.K. and the U.S. Thus in 1982, construction was completed on a new Animal Health Research Center at Terre Haute for field trials. Also during this time, Pfizer created, on a much smaller scale than Euroclin, what might be called "Eurovet" for carrying out field trials on animals in Europe. The capability was also developed to supervise field trials in Latin America, Africa, Australia and Japan. These capabilities were crucial to the successful development of Terramycin/LA and the Paratect bolus.

Organizationally a structure was created which at the time was unique within Central Research. Curt Askelson and Tim Cronin, both located in Groton, were made responsible for all Development and Discovery Research carried out in the U.S. and U.K. respectively. Project teams comprised U.S. and U.K. members; joint quarterly project reviews were held; and transatlantic communications; trips and personnel exchanges took place at an unprecedented level. Agricultural Products R&D truly became one organization – not two organizations under the same head. At the same time, regular meetings were held with both U.S. and International Marketing, principally to

keep them informed of and to solicit their inputs on R&D plans and progress.

During the last four years of Conover's tenure, approval was finally obtained for significant staff increases, and numerous staff were redeployed from Development and Market Support to Discovery Research. In 1979, Agricultural Products R&D had 153 people – actually two less than in 1975 – but by 1983, the total had grown to 186, and the number of people in Discovery had increased from 62 to 127. Research projects and strategies begun in this period were to reach fruition by the end of the decade.

In 1984, Curt Askelson succeeded Conover as senior vice president while Tim Cronin remained vice president for Discovery Research. Cronin's unified and enlarged organization hit pay dirt with three new drugs in three different therapeutic areas – all within the space of 18 months. In recognition of the focus on products to treat animals, the Agricultural Products R&D Division was renamed Animal Health R&D.

One of the new drugs is Advocin (danofloxacin), a broad-spectrum fluoroquinolone antibacterial that has been especially effective in treating respiratory and enteric diseases in cattle,

Liquamycin LA-200 was the name given to Terramycin/LA in the United States and Canada. The drug was incorporated in a solution that was slowly absorbed over three or four days, allowing farmers to substitute a convenient single dose for repeated daily injections.

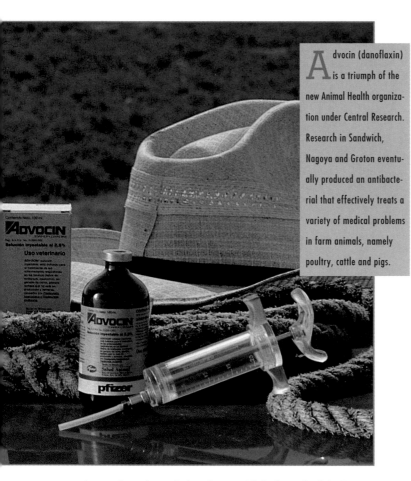

Advocin (danoflaxin) is a triumph of the new Animal Health organization under Central Research. Research in Sandwich, Nagoya and Groton eventually produced an antibacterial that effectively treats a variety of medical problems in farm animals, namely poultry, cattle and pigs.

swine and poultry. It has been widely launched in Japan and many other countries, including many in Latin America; these will be followed by Europe and Canada. Advocin's development, credited to Tom Schaaf, who headed the discovery team, and Paul McGuirk, the lead chemist, is a good example of rational drug design where the structure of the molecule was logically modified to eliminate an undesirable activity, mutagenesis.

The second drug is Aviax (semduramicin), for the treatment of coccidiosis, a parasitic disease common in broiler chickens and caged-laying hens. The discovery of this drug is a superb example of teamwork among scientists in Groton, Nagoya and Sandwich. It followed from a strategic decision made in the early eighties to emphasize microbial metabolite screening as a source of animal health drugs – especially coccidiostats. A precursor to the drug, UK-58,852, was discovered from screening in Nagoya, but it failed on toxicological grounds during development in Groton.

"Based on available structure/activity information, we decided to improve toleration of this ionophore by removing one of its sugar groups," says Alex Goudie, now vice president of Animal Health Discovery. The resulting derivative (semduramicin) proved to be not only safe but also highly effective.

Following heroic efforts, the Groton Fermentation Group developed a high-yielding process for its manufacture directly from the fermentation broth. Coupled with Pfizer's licensed anti-coccidial Coxistac (salinomycin), Aviax should make Pfizer a leading marketer of products to control poultry disease.

The third – and potentially the biggest – of the three new drugs is Dectomax (doramectin), a potent broad-spectrum endectocide for controlling internal and external parasites in livestock, including worms, ticks, mites, lice and flies. It goes head-to-head against Ivomec, a Merck product that is one of a class of compounds known as avermectins. "We said we wanted a superior product and we got one," says Tim Cronin, now senior vice president, Animal Health R&D.

Ideas for generating new avermectins had been discussed for some time between Mike Leeming's group and Chemical Products in Sandwich. The specific idea which led to doramectin started in 1982, when Kelvin Holdom began a student collaboration with Manchester University. His research proposal was to look at the feasibility of producing, via fermentation, an unnatural avermectin by feeding cyclobutyl carboxylic acid to the avermectin-producing microorganism.

The initial effort showed no signs of success, and so the outside project was bolstered by in-house research which extended the feeding experiments to many alternative substrates. "We fed cyclohexyl carboxylic acid to the fermentation broth," Alex Goudie recalls, "and examined the broth a few days later. The place went wild when we identified a new peak on the chromatogram and we isolated the first 60 micrograms of our new avermectin. The process for Dectomax started with very low yields, and great credit goes to the Groton Fermentation Group for scaling it up and making it economically viable. Dectomax has superior properties over competitive agents: it kills a broader spectrum of parasites and lasts longer, providing protection against reinfection."

In November 1994, Pfizer announced that it was buying the animal health business of SmithKline Beecham P.L.C. of Britain for $1.45 billion in cash. As a result of the agreement, Pfizer has become the largest maker of drugs for animals, overtaking Merck and Co. and accounting for about one-tenth of the $12 billion global market. The move also gives Pfizer an entry into the major market of drugs for pets.

Food Science

One of the ways Central Research has ensured adequate returns on its growing R&D investment is by maintaining diverse research goals. Practically since its beginnings, Pfizer had been a chemical company serving the food industry, producing such things as citric acid, tartaric acid, ascorbic acid and vitamins in bulk in what was then called the Chemical Division and later Specialty Chemicals. In the early 1970s, a decision was made to expand the company's base, to branch out from food into industrial products.

One major project was to develop water treatment chemicals for desalination – the recovery of fresh water from sea water. It was driven largely by petrodollars in the Middle East. To the Arabs, water was worth more

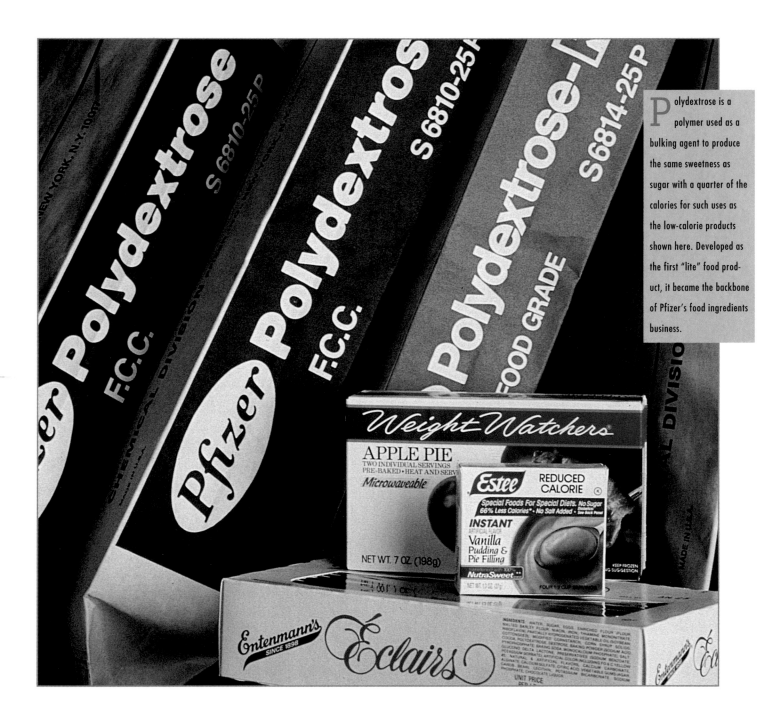

Polydextrose is a polymer used as a bulking agent to produce the same sweetness as sugar with a quarter of the calories for such uses as the low-calorie products shown here. Developed as the first "lite" food product, it became the backbone of Pfizer's food ingredients business.

than oil, and at the very high prices oil was commanding in those days, they could afford to spend a lot of money on desalination. Pfizer perfected chemicals to prevent the build-up of scale on the heat exchanger walls of big fresh-water recovery plants, and that evolved into a related business for scale control in reverse osmosis, the other method of producing fresh water from sea water.

Another opportunity Pfizer saw was for enhanced-recovery chemicals in oil production, also driven by the high value of oil in those days. As oil fields become depleted, the oil they yield contains increasing quantities of water. Central Research developed a number of polymers and gelants that could be pumped into the ground to enhance oil recovery by retarding water flow.

Both of these efforts came a cropper when the price of oil collapsed in 1986. It was no longer attractive to use these chemicals or the procedures, both of which were costly. The businesses were sold, and these lines of research were shut down.

Fortunately, Pfizer had not abandoned its interest in food chemicals. One of the products it had been working on was polydextrose, a polymer used as a bulking agent to produce sugar with a

A taste panel at Pfizer's research laboratories tests the effects of the properties of Veltol and Veltol-Plus in a gelatin dessert. These flavor enhancers put Pfizer in the front-running position in the world market.

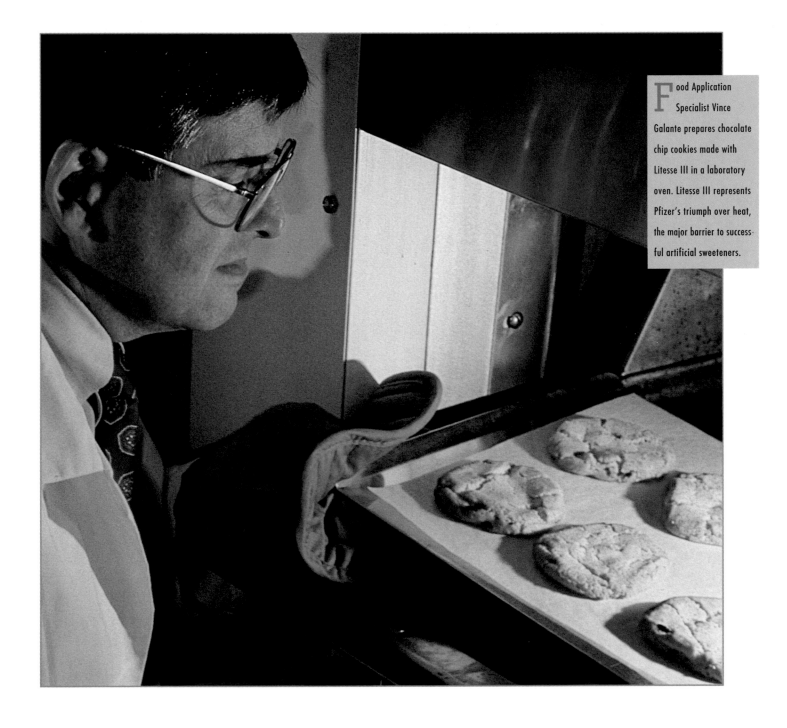

Food Application Specialist Vince Galante prepares chocolate chip cookies made with Litesse III in a laboratory oven. Litesse III represents Pfizer's triumph over heat, the major barrier to successful artificial sweeteners.

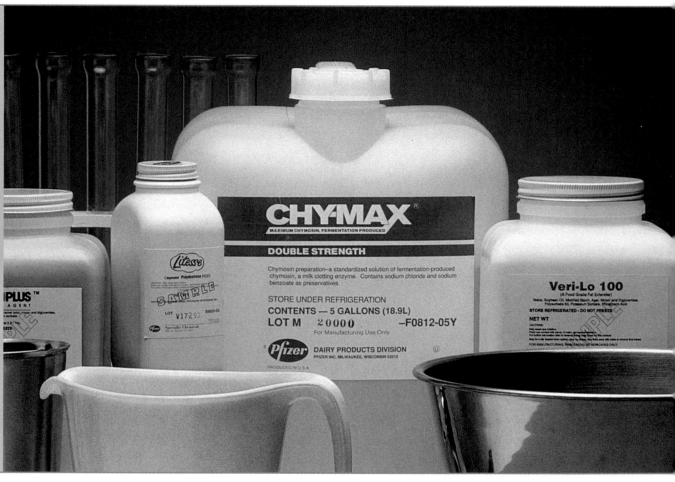

An array of Pfizer food products includes Chy-Max, a natural fermentation-derived cheese coagulant. The first recombinant DNA product approved for food use by the FDA, Chy-Max represented Pfizer's leadership in the biotech industry. Pfizer had beaten out every premiere biotech company with the introduction of the new product.

quarter of the calories for such applications as low-calorie ice cream. Polydextrose had been developed in Groton back in the 1960s under the supervision of Charles Stephens, with Hans Rennhard obtaining the patent. It was a pioneering step – the first "lite" food product – and the safety testing took a long time. After protracted negotiations with the FDA, the product was finally approved in 1981 and became the backbone of Pfizer's food ingredients business.

As extensions of polydextrose, the company developed three subsequent forms. Litesse, introduced in 1991, eliminates a slight off-taste in the original due to a trace ingredient and can be used in delicate foods where taste is critical. Litesse II, an acid-free and bitter-free form aimed largely at confectionery use, was introduced in 1993. Recently, in Japan, Pfizer launched Litesse III, a fourth-generation product that is a color-stable and heat-stable form of polydextrose; it will not caramelize and turn brown when cooked and thus is particularly suited to hard-candy manufacturing and as a tabletop sweetener.

One of the products that has made the Food Group Science proudest is Chy-Max (chymosin), a natural product that is the first recombinant DNA product approved for food use by the FDA.

Studies had indicated that the dairy industry would face a critical shortage of natural calf rennet (obtained from the stomachs of suckling calves) by 1990. Ken Harewood, a molecular biologist with Central Research in Groton, proposed that he obtain from calves' stomachs the gene that codes for the production of chymosin and insert it in a bacterial strain called *E. coli* K-12, a microbial workhorse used to produce insulin and growth hormones. It was the job of Art Franke, the project leader, to manipulate the bacteria into expressing chymosin, "cutting and pasting" DNA to get the genetic sequence that would provide high levels of the enzyme.

At the time, some 20 other companies were working on chymosin, using the same approach and the same bacterium. "Genentech, the premier biotech company in the United States, finally told us they had abandoned the project," says Richard Hinman, former senior vice president of Chemical Products R&D, now retired. "They said they gave it up probably for the same reasons that we would; it just isn't economically viable. Meanwhile we knew that we had broken its back. That was pretty exciting, beating out those other guys, who had all the molecular biologists and genetic engineers in the world. Where we succeeded was not in the genetic engineering – everyone could do that as well as we could – but in taking the old fermentation know-how that we had and scaling it up through the pilot plant and getting the bug to make chymosin in a practical way."

The work of research chemist Ting Po I led to a full-scale fermentation recovery process for chymosin, which was tested out in Pfizer's pilot plant in Groton. Then came the moment of truth – a cheese-tasting party. "We did a blind test, sampling cheeses made with animal-derived and fermentation-derived chymosin," Franke recalls. "It was impossible to tell which was which. To me that was a real thrill – the final chapter of years of work. And it was an aged cheddar, a very tasty cheese."

Chy-Max was filed with the FDA in December 1987 and received approval in 1990 in the record time of two and a half years. "Everyone was for biotechnology, and the United States had to be in the lead – couldn't let it slip away to the Germans or the Japanese," says Hinman. "We built a plant to make Chy-Max in Terre Haute, and it's been expanded three times since."

On another front, the great success of Nutrasweet prompted Pfizer to seek a superior low-calorie sweetener. The result was Alitame. It is a high-potency product: whereas Nutrasweet is 350 times as sweet as sugar, Alitame is 2,000 times sweeter – a pound of it is equal to a ton of sugar. Nutrasweet, moreover, is not stable in the heat of the process used to bake cakes; Alitame, on the other hand, is heat-stable. To arrive at a candidate, the discovery team modified the structure of Nutrasweet into 200 different compounds, finally picking the one that combined high sweetness with ease of manufacture.

"It was a close call," says Dick Hinman. "The management wanted to stop the sweetener discovery program, which hadn't come up with anything in two or three years. Strictly speaking we should have been closing it down, but Charlie Stephens and I agreed that we had something interesting. So we kept it going without saying anything, and at the last minute we discovered Alitame."

Alitame was discovered by Mike Hendrick in 1981 and submitted to the FDA in 1987, after lengthy testing. It recently received its first international approvals in Australia, New Zealand, Mexico and China.

"Food additives are a very tough row to hoe," says Hinman. "The regulatory restraints on a new material to be put into the food chain are very high – worse in many ways than the pharmaceutical business – because there are all the issues of safety, but no benefits, like you get with drugs, along with the risks. When we get Alitame on the market, however, its potency will give us a great cost benefit; it will be cheaper than Nutrasweet or Aspartame. It could be really big."

In early 1993, the name of the division was changed from Specialty Chemicals to Food Science, reflecting a rededication to supplying healthful, high-value food ingredients. Its research and development arm, consisting of some 75 people, was headed by Dave Trecker, senior vice president, who ticks off other products on the line or in the works:

"For our brewing ingredients business, we have devised processes to make synthetic hop products that provide the requisite bitterness to beer: Isohop, RediHop and, most recently, TetraHop. We are also in the process of significantly upgrading the manufacture of our flavor enhancers, Veltol and Veltol-Plus, where we have a world-leading position.

"A major thrust right now is fat substitutes, the single biggest opportunity in food ingredients today. For low-temperature applications like salad dressings, we devised Veri-Lo, an emulsion designed to 'fool the mouth' into thinking that a little fat is a lot of fat. We recently licensed Solatrim, a family of reduced-calorie triglycerides, from Nabisco and are developing them for a host of food uses, initially cocoa butter replacements for chocolate. An exciting new research discovery is Sorbestrin, in this case designed for the baking and frying markets, a huge untapped potential.

"Another promising new area is 'natural' food additives, drawing on the growing consumer trend toward natural foods. To capitalize on this, high-throughput screening, adapted from our pharmaceutical techniques, is being applied to extracts of foods and food processing streams from around the world. Initial targets are natural antioxidants and anti-microbials to prevent food spoilage.

"Our overall research is directed toward strengthening our existing product line and bringing down costs – the food business is very cost-conscious – as well as developing entirely new products," concludes Trecker. "The Pfizer pipeline of new food ingredients is richer than at any time in our history. With 80 percent of adult Americans consuming low-calorie and reduced-fat foods and beverages, it's a very big market indeed."

Food Science has made many valuable contributions to Pfizer goals over the years and has several successful projects launched or in development. However, corporate management decided in 1995 to focus Pfizer more sharply on health-oriented businesses. Consequently, Pfizer's Food Science business was sold in January 1996 to the Finnish nutrition company, Cultor, Ltd.

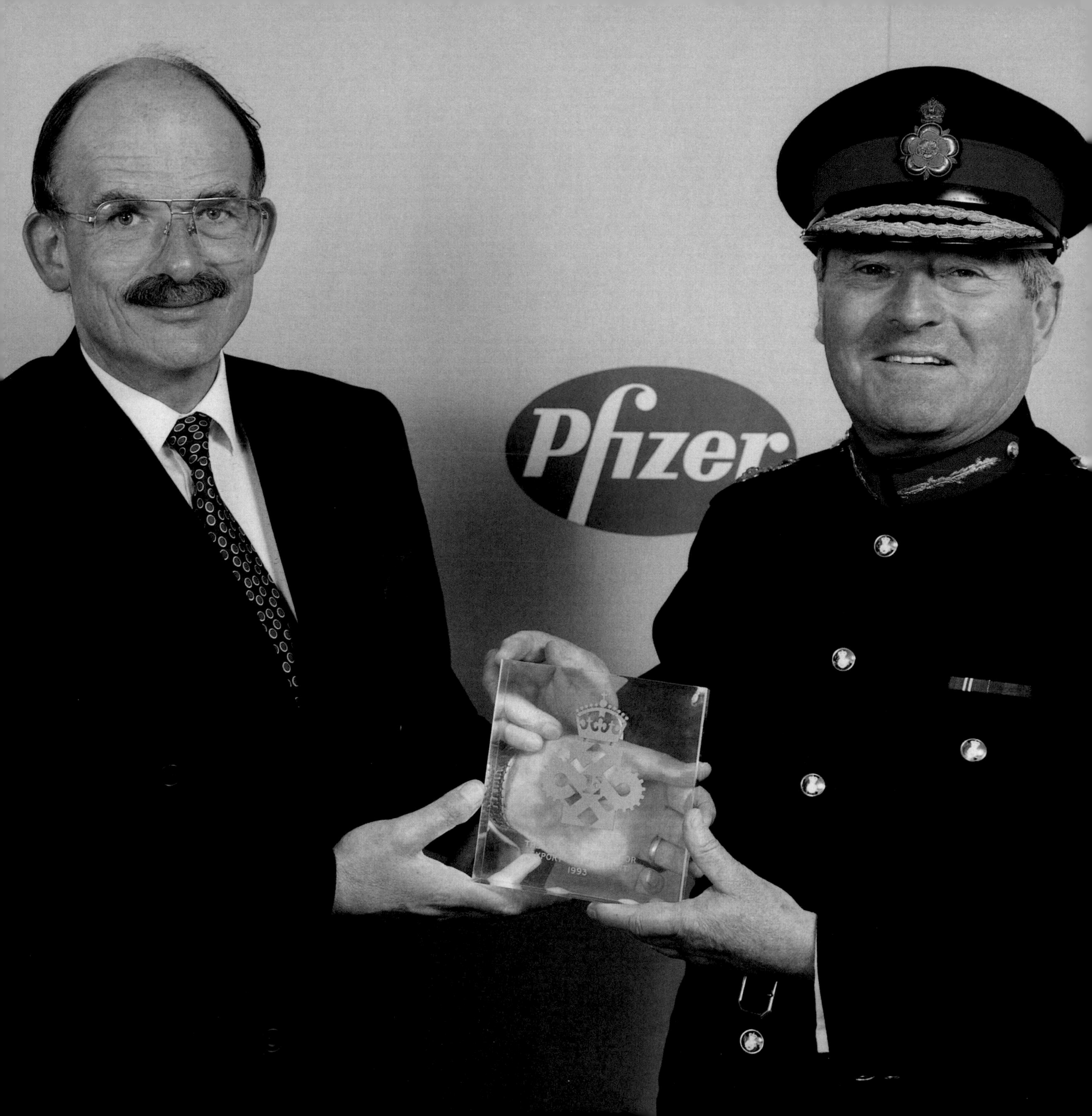
Pfizer
1993

CHAPTER EIGHT

Diflucan: Case Study of a Drug

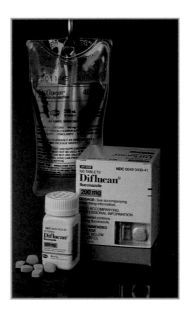

Hugh O' Connor, chairman of Pfizer Ltd, Sandwich, left, accepts the Queen's Award for Technological Achievement in 1993 for the export of Trosyl, Terramycin and anthelmintics. This was Sandwich's third Queen's Award; the first came for the development of Mansil in 1979, the second for Diflucan in 1991. At right, Diflucan is shown in pill and injectable forms.

When Diflucan won the Queen's Award for Science and Technology in 1991, Ken Richardson, its inventor, was invited to Buckingham Palace to receive the honor. His daughter, all excited, instructed him to report carefully on what the Queen looked like and what she wore. "I was looking at her so hard, trying to remember, that I forgot to bow," Richardson recalls with a chuckle. "So when I went on to meet the Duke of Kent, I gave him a tremendous bow to make up for it."

Richardson's trip to Buckingham Palace was 20 years in the making. He was a young man working in Groton when the antifungal program got started at Sandwich in 1970, a year after he had joined Pfizer. It was something that had been urged by Sheldon Gilgore, then head of Pfizer's Pharmaceutical Products Division. A medical doctor, Gilgore foresaw that there would be a growing incidence of serious fungal infections with advances in modern medicine, that resistance would emerge to current treatments (just as it does to bacteria) and that new drugs would be needed to combat them. Gilgore's "brilliant insight," as Barry Bloom describes it, worked out very much the way it was forecast. Says Bloom, "Shelley deserves credit for having made a great crystal-ball prediction almost 15 years before the emergence of AIDS, which lent new urgency to the problem."

The program began modestly, with not much to report for two or three years. Then in 1973, Pfizer heard about a new class of compounds called imidazoles that had been developed by Janssen, a Belgian company that is now part of Johnson & Johnson. The compounds were effective against fungus infections,

but they worked only when placed topically on the skin in the form of a powder or paste. Sandwich scientists started looking for an imidazole that would work orally, when taken as a tablet. The result, after much work, was a compound named tioconazole, which Pfizer Ltd marketed in Europe as Trosyl. It worked topically, but still not very well orally. In 1978, the company decided to put a new team of chemists on the problem and take another look. This was when Ken Richardson, who had transferred over to Sandwich in 1974, was made responsible for the project.

There were two things wrong with the molecules the team was working with: they were vulnerable to metabolism, and the little bit that got through the liver produced very low blood levels of the drug. The reason for the latter, the re-

1991

**AWARDED TO
CENTRAL RESEARCH
DIVISION OF PFIZER LIMITED**

The culmination of the Diflucan research project effort came after 20 years, when Ken Richardson accepted the Queen's Award for Diflucan — the most prescribed antifungal drug in the world.

searchers found, was that the molecules were lipophilic, or fat-loving; they stuck to fatty tissues and to proteins in the blood, so that the actual amount of drug available to attack the fungus was minuscule.

"It was incredibly frustrating," says Richardson. "We could take small steps, but we couldn't make the big jump we were looking for. We were at least two years behind Janssen." At this point, Richardson realized they hadn't tried changing a particular part of the molecule; they had never altered the imidazole part because everyone thought that was absolutely essential. So he gave Bill Million a list of 20 different groups to put in place of the imidazole. Nineteen proved to have no activity whatsoever. The twentieth, called a triazole, was a breakthrough. When the team tested the compound, they found that, while it was four or five times less active in the test tube, it was three times more active in animals.

But there was still something wrong with one portion of the molecule, so in May 1981, the researchers tried the same triazole on the right as well as the left side of the molecule. "It was the most dramatic compound I've ever seen in my life," says Richardson. "It was absolutely stunning. We'd been looking for something that was perhaps five times better than the Janssen compound when we put it into animals. This compound, UK-47,265, was a *hundred* times better. We patented it, made more of it, and put it into development the very next month. Then we sent it over to Amboise for safety testing in animals." After about three months, the team got bad news. The compound proved extremely liver-toxic, and it caused cleft palates in the offspring of rats that were pregnant during testing. For all intents and purposes, the compound was dead. "It was a bad moment for us, but we weren't too worried because we had made some similar derivatives over the past three months," says Richardson. "We sent 10 more compounds over to Amboise. Nine of them turned out to be bad. The tenth wasn't liver-toxic, but it wasn't anywhere near as active — about 10 times better than Janssen's compound instead of 100 times."

The researchers made two or three more structural changes on the nontoxic compound and sent them to Amboise around Christmas, 1981. One of them, UK-49,858, proved to be non-liver-toxic and not teratogenic in rats. Moreover, it was 100 times more active than Janssen's compound. The team named it fluconazole, later to be given the trademark Diflucan.

Two months later, again bad news accompanied the good. It turned out that ICI, the big British pharmaceu-

Bill Million was Ken Richardson's collaborator in the invention of Diflucan. Its development was a series of false starts, high hopes and crashing disappointments before compound UK-49,858 finally panned out. The inventors named it fluconazole, which was later given the trade name Diflucan.

tical company, had beaten Pfizer to the class of compounds with two triazoles on them, which they had patented. But where Pfizer had gone on beyond UK-47,265, ICI had given up because all their compounds had been very toxic or very weak. Because of the unique properties of fluconazole Pfizer received a patent on it, but the company still had to pay ICI a license fee because of ICI's earlier broad patent.

In March 1982, fluconazole went into development. In clinical trials in man, it proved to have excellent oral absorption and yielded high blood levels following one dose a day. Since fluconazole was water-loving rather than fat-loving, it could be given not only orally but also intravenously, a major advantage in very sick patients and those in a coma who cannot take oral drugs.

Fluconazole worked on patients with skin infections, athlete's foot and ringworm. It also cured women with vaginal infections — one oral capsule delivered enough drug to stay in their bodies a whole week, providing antifungal activity all the time. Pfizer thought it had a fine product for superficial, nuisance infections and planned to market it as such.

At this point, however, disagreement cropped up. Central Research had its own ideas about how to position fluconazole; Pfizer Roerig, which was going to sell it in the United States, had different ideas; Pfizer International, which was going to sell it around the world, had still other ideas.

That was when John Niblack had the idea of the Advanced Candidate Management Team (ACMT). He, Karen Katen (then vice president of marketing for Pfizer's Roerig Division) and Joe Lombardino worked closely to form the prototype team around fluconazole. Appointed as chairman was Lyn Wiesinger, who worked in New Product Planning at Roerig.

The Advanced Candidate Management Team met regularly, and was instrumental in achieving interdivisional agreement on how to design the clinical program to test fluconazole. It also put the NDA together for submission to the Food and Drug Administration. The experiment worked so well that Lombardino formed ACMTs for all of Pfizer's advanced compounds from that time on. The concept of using interdivisional teams to plan, monitor and report on advanced (Phase III) candidates has now become institutionalized at Pfizer.

In the early 1980s, as Pfizer was still developing fluconazole, a new specter appeared on the horizon — the epidemic of AIDS. Very soon it became evident that AIDS patients, because of their compromised immune systems, were susceptible to a whole host of infectious

A Pfizer sales representative studies a training manual on Diflucan, preparing to call on doctors to describe its many advantages.

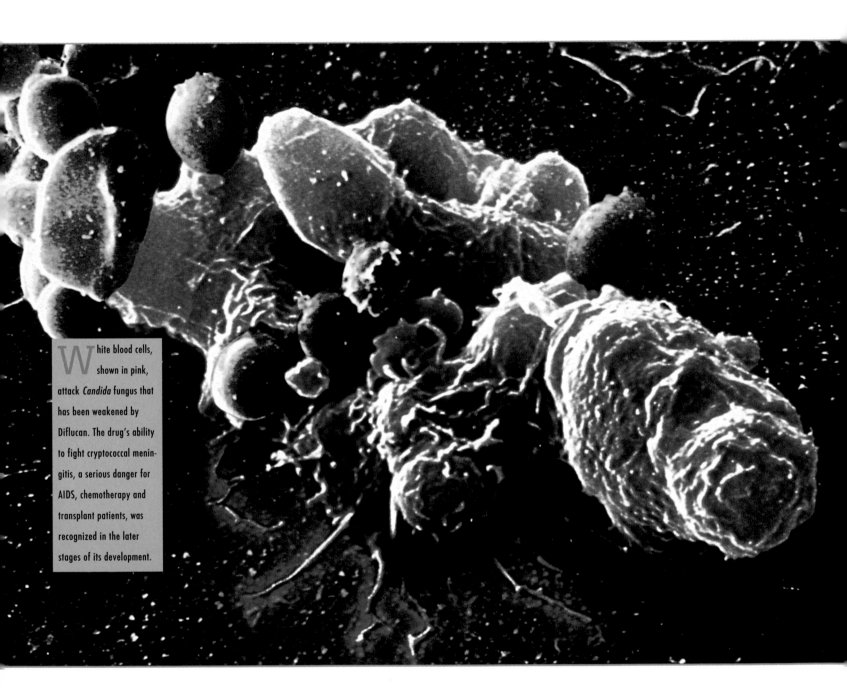

White blood cells, shown in pink, attack *Candida* fungus that has been weakened by Diflucan. The drug's ability to fight cryptococcal meningitis, a serious danger for AIDS, chemotherapy and transplant patients, was recognized in the later stages of its development.

diseases, including common fungal infections like candida. Less common but deadly was cryptococcal meningitis, an infection of the lining of the brain to which AIDS patients are particularly vulnerable. The fungus is normally fought off by a healthy person's immune system. Persons with damaged immune systems — not only AIDS patients, but those undergoing chemotherapy for cancer or organ transplant recipients — cannot fight off infections, and if cryptococcus gets into the brain, the result is invariably death.

At the time, the only drug available to treat life-threatening fungal infections was amphotericin B, which had to be dripped into the bloodstream over a period of hours every day. It usually did the job but at a dreadful cost in side effects — fever, chills, nausea, abnormally low blood pressure, shock, organ damage, kidney toxicity. AIDS patients had a name for it: "amphoterrible."

Pfizer's clinical researchers reasoned that fluconazole might be an effective treatment against candida infections and cryptococcal meningitis. When they tested the hypothesis by giving the drug to patients with these infections, the results were magical: the infections would just vanish. "In some cases AIDS patients were in comas and were expected to die," says Richardson. "The next day they would be out of their coma, sitting up in

bed, and a week later they would be out of the hospital. The drug really rescued them from death's door."

"All of a sudden it lit a light bulb in the marketing divisions in New York as well as the research people in Groton," says Jeffrey Stritar, M.D., Groton's executive director of Clinical Research. Stritar captained fluconazole's development in the United States through the extensive clinical trials of Phase III. "They said, 'Hey, wait a minute, we're going in the wrong direction. Not only is there an unmet medical need where we can do a great service, but it's become a far greater commercial opportunity than this other stuff we've been fiddling around with for four or five years.'"

Pfizer wasn't the only one who recognized the challenge. In 1987, the FDA had set up a separate division to expedite the development of new drugs for AIDS. At the urging of the FDA — which agreed that a drug like fluconazole comes along once in a decade, if that — Pfizer temporarily suspended studies of superficial infections and concentrated only on serious ones, primarily in AIDS patients. Data were collected from some 5,500 patients in all, about 1,500 of them with serious infections.

While clinical studies were still going on, a groundswell of demand for the new drug began to appear. By the end of 1989, Pfizer was receiving 25 to 30

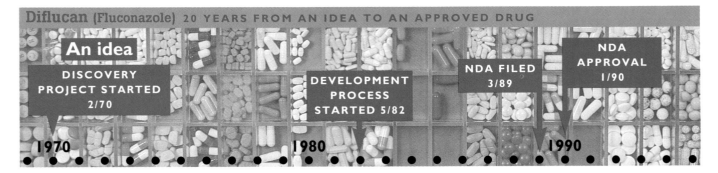

Diflucan (Fluconazole) 20 YEARS FROM AN IDEA TO AN APPROVED DRUG

An idea

DISCOVERY PROJECT STARTED 2/70

DEVELOPMENT PROCESS STARTED 5/82

NDA FILED 3/89

NDA APPROVAL 1/90

1970   1980   1990

phone calls a day from physicians who wanted to use it on their patients. In response, the company set up a compassionate-treatment program, under which more than 2,300 patients who had exhausted conventional treatment received the unapproved drug under the control of the FDA.

In the space of little more than a year and a half, the company started and concluded the clinical trials that led to FDA approval of fluconazole for treatment of candida infections and cryptococcal meningitis. It received approval 10 months after the New Drug Application was submitted — certainly the shortest time for approval in recent Pfizer history and among the shortest for any drug. Fluconazole, with the trade name Diflucan, went on the market in the United Kingdom, Ireland and France in September 1988. It was approved for sale in the United States in January 1990.

Diflucan is already the most-prescribed antifungal drug in the world, and its future looks bright. In addition to patients with AIDS and those undergoing chemotherapy, it can be used on patients who are on long-term therapy with drugs that depress the immune system. The drug was recently approved for use as a prophylaxis against the emergence of fungal infections in bone-marrow transplant patients, whose immune systems have been compromised. Also approved is an oral suspension dosage form that can be used by patients who have a hard time swallowing a pill, and a claim for using Diflucan to treat vaginitis.

Scott Hopkins, group director of Clinical Research at Groton, sums it up: "Diflucan is a groundbreaking drug that people will remember for years to come."

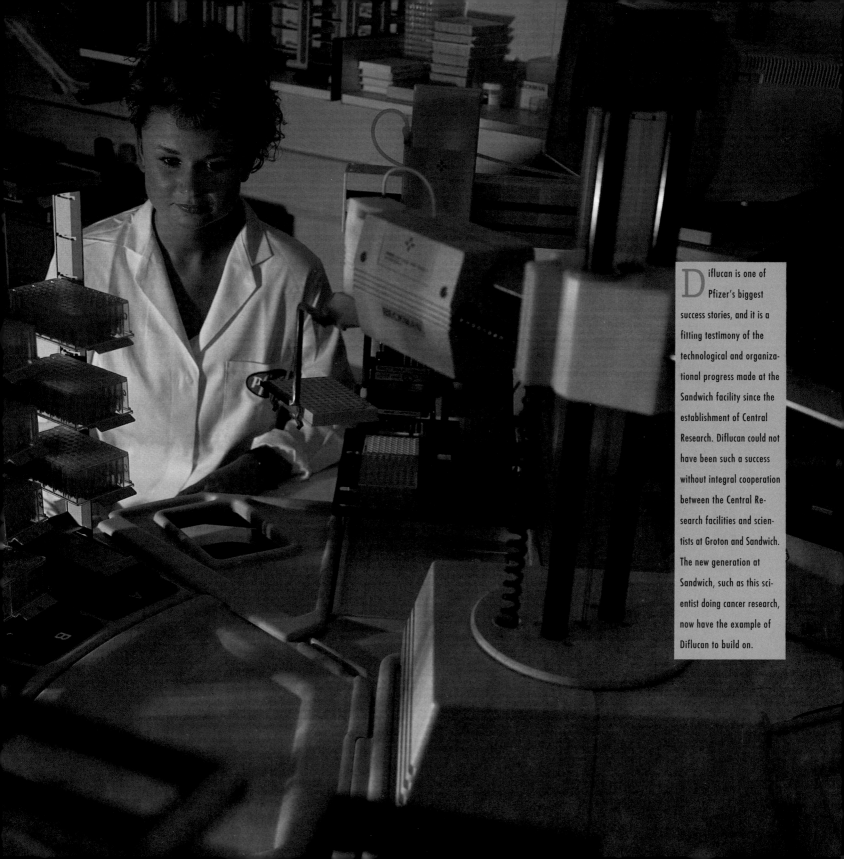

Diflucan is one of Pfizer's biggest success stories, and it is a fitting testimony of the technological and organizational progress made at the Sandwich facility since the establishment of Central Research. Diflucan could not have been such a success without integral cooperation between the Central Research facilities and scientists at Groton and Sandwich. The new generation at Sandwich, such as this scientist doing cancer research, now have the example of Diflucan to build on.

an avid interest in art with his growing interest in the biological sciences. In his final year, he was awarded the Francis Bacon scholarship, named after the sixteenth-century English philosopher and scientist who saw a oneness between the arts and sciences.

Ringrose took his Ph.D. at Cambridge as well, finishing with a Ph.D. thesis on the mechanism of action of protein antibiotics called bacteriocins and how they destroyed DNA inside target cells. He was particularly

meet, he pumped gasoline evenings at a local filling station in Cambridge.

Rather than pursuing an academic career – he had offers to teach from Cambridge as well as Tufts University in Boston – Ringrose decided to do something practical and work to discover new medicines. In 1970 he joined the laboratories of Hoffman LaRoche in the U.K. and subsequently in the U.S. and worked in infectious diseases and inflammation until 1979, moving up the ladder

Peter S. Ringrose

Peter Ringrose, senior vice president of European R&D at Sandwich and worldwide head of Discovery, was going to school in Leicester in central England in the mid-1950s when his interest in science was triggered by organic chemistry. "I became fascinated with the chemistry of life, what it was that transformed dead, organic molecules into living, thinking beings. Like other budding scientists, when I was 9 or 10, I had a chemistry set in my parents' garage, making a lot of smells and often explosive mixtures."

Ringrose went on to Corpus Christi College at Cambridge University, where he majored in biochemistry and molecular biology, graduating in 1967. He won one of the college's coveted prizes with an essay on the chemical nature of natural colors, combining

influenced by a number of Nobel prize winners who were lecturing at Cambridge at the time, including Francis Crick, who co-discovered the structure of DNA in the 1950s. While still in college, Ringrose married his childhood sweetheart, Nancy; to make ends

to become head of Biochemistry .

He moved in 1979 to the Sandoz Institute of Infectious Diseases in Vienna, Austria, where he became fluent in German, but largely because of concerns about his children's education and attracted by an offer from Ian Wrigley – then head of Pfizer's research operation at Sandwich – he moved back to the U.K. in 1982. He was recruited to head up the Discovery Biology Group and to take charge of all medicinal projects. In 1986 he became overall head of Sandwich Discovery, reporting to Alan Wilson, who had taken over from Wrigley. In 1992 when Wilson retired, Ringrose became head of Sandwich Research and Development and in 1994 also became head of Worldwide Discovery.

When he joined Pfizer, there hadn't really been any drug candidates that had been discovered in Sandwich that had gone on to become significant products, and the future of Sandwich was at that time somewhat in question. In the year that he joined, fluconazole (Diflucan) and amlodipine (Norvasc) were nominated for development and were followed by a rich pipeline of U.K.-discovered drugs. The most notable of those is dofetilide, an antiarrythmic agent, which Ringrose helped set up as a project. Other compounds he has been closely associated with are darifenacin, for urinary incontinence and irritable bowel syndrome (IBS), which is now moving toward full-scale development, as well as others in the cardiovascular, antifungal, pulmonary, urogenital and impotence areas. "We must have over 15 U.K.-discovered compounds that are in various stages of development," he says. "So I feel I've played some part in making Sandwich as productive as it now is." In the 13 years since he joined the company, Sandwich has trebled in size, in terms of both buildings and people; the staff of 450 has grown to almost 1,500.

Ringrose points to the restructured project teams and new research areas he helped initiate in the 1980s, chaired by research scientists and assisted by project coordinators. He helped redesign the Project Operating Plans (POPS) and started the

Preliminary Candidate Report for alerting the development operations when a new candidate was ready to make the transition from discovery to development. The focus and emphasis on making the Sandwich operation more productive and innovative has changed much during Ringrose's tenure. He has clearly left his mark on Sandwich research operations; many of the candidates in the Pfizer pipeline today came from projects he helped start years ago.

Ringrose lives just outside of Canterbury in a hamlet with the picturesque name of Lynsore Bottom in a round-towered seven-

teenth-century house built out of flint, which was once used for drying hops for beer. He and his wife raise sheep and chickens on six acres of farm. His hobbies include skiing, horseback-riding, scuba diving, and playing badminton and squash ("until my two sons started to beat me without breaking into a sweat"). He relaxes by painting, reading nineteenth-century literature and listening to music ranging from the Beatles to Mahler.

Peter Ringrose, currently worldwide head of Discovery Research and responsible for the Sandwich R&D operation, has spent 13 years making Sandwich a stronger, more productive facility. At the bottom of the opposite page, he is shown with Hugh O'Connor, chairman of Pfizer Ltd, and Virginia Bottomley, Secretary of Health of the United Kingdom, at Sandwich's 40th anniversary.

9

Carol Marzetta welcomes
Claudia Turner to the finish
line of the Pfizer triathlon.
Slowed by an injury during
the race, Claudia was the
last one to cross it, but her
Pfizer colleagues all stayed
to cheer on her determina-
tion to complete the race.
The triathlon, just one more
opportunity for Central
Research employees to show
their dedication and spirit,
has been held every year
for nearly a decade on Eastern Point Beach in Groton.
With a relay option, participation in the 400-yard
swim, 10-mile bike and
5-mile run has increased.

CHAPTER NINE

The Soul of a Company

"We have a record of being very aggressive," says Ed Pratt, former Pfizer Inc CEO. "And yet we are a company that has a soul."

This "soul" shows in many ways, from the company's extraordinary generosity in giving to the United Way to its provision of free drugs to the needy and victims of national disasters.

Central Research Reaching Out to the Community

Pfizer shows its concern by becoming involved in helping to solve the major problems facing American education today. The company's involvement started six years ago when Ed Pratt was chairman of the Business Roundtable, an organization of leading businessmen, at one of whose meetings it was suggested that corporations could be doing more to help kindergarten through twelfth-grade education. Pratt formed a Pfizer committee, headed by Don Farley, now President of Consumer Health Care Group, which came up with a primary focus on encouraging kids in middle schools – a critical time in their lives – to get interested in science and math.

One member of the committee, Dick Hinman of Central Research, became so fascinated by the challenge that he stayed on after retirement to coordinate the efforts of Pfizer volunteers at 15 manufacturing and distribution sites around the country and in Puerto Rico.

"There are various levels of activity," says Hinman. "At some sites it's modest: they run tours of the plant and send some speakers into classrooms. At others it's extensive: they give scholarship awards, hold science fairs, offer internships for teachers to learn what goes on in industry and what practical science is all about. All told, [1995] we reach some 500 science and math teachers and 20,000 students a year, 5,000 of them in the Groton area alone. And we now have a companion initiative in Sandwich, reaching some 2,000 additional students."

The program in Groton, which began in 1988, is called SMART ("Science and Math are Really Terrific").

Even retirement can't stop Dick Hinman, senior vice president for Chemical Products R&D until 1992, from helping teach children the importance and fun of math and science. He was one of the original organizers and is still leading "SMART," a mentoring program for Connecticut schoolchildren near Central Research headquarters in Groton.

It involves middle-school students from grades five through eight at 11 different schools in southeastern Connecticut and a total of nearly 300 Pfizer volunteers.

"The scientists who work at Central Research are an absolutely extraordinary resource for the local education community," says the program's leader, David Burnett, director of Employee Resources. "They are people who earn their living doing science and math. As such, they are spectacular role models for children. They're able to go to classrooms and not just talk about things, but actually do them."

The Pfizer researchers in Groton, Connecticut, are available to speak and put on classroom demonstrations on more than 50 topics. Workshops are held to instruct teachers in the use of hands-on teaching materials, which they take back to their classrooms in the form of teaching kits. Pfizer also underwrites travel funds to allow teachers to attend professional workshops. Mini-grants of up to $2,000 are awarded to schools to enable them to purchase special equipment, and Pfizer refurbishes science classrooms at needy schools. Perhaps most valuable of all, the company hires several teachers a year to work in

Arthur Girard ... eron, Roberta Faiella an...

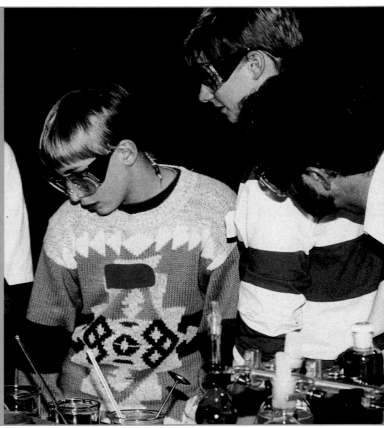

The Science and Math Jamboree ("SAM-JAM"), part of the SMART program, is held for two days every January by Groton research volunteers at the field house of Connecticut College in nearby New London. Some 200 Pfizer employees educate and entertain 2,000 eighth-graders with demonstrations, including a live appearance by Anton van Leeuwenhoek, the inventor of the microscope, played by Arthur Girard.

its laboratories for six weeks as summer interns, offering them an inside view of research, development and quality control and sending them back to their classrooms with new insights to use in teaching their students.

The highlight of the program each year is a Science and Math Jamboree ("SAMJAM"), a two-day event held in January in the cavernous field house of Connecticut College in New London. Some 2,000 eighth-graders attend to witness demonstrations by 200

or more Pfizer volunteers. The presentations range from extracting DNA from onion cells to illustrating the probability theory with loaded dice.

A favorite demonstrator is Arthur Girard, a Central Research microbiologist who dresses up as Anton van Leeuwenhoek, a seventeenth-century Dutchman who invented the microscope. Girard astounds the kids by showing them a replica of that crude device, then swabs the inside of a student's mouth and puts the swab in a team, with a more than respectable handicap of five.

After graduation and an internship, Saxton served as a research fellow at Leeds University, specializing in cardiovascular disease. Then followed five exciting years with the Royal Air Force's Institute of Aviation Medicine, researching the effects of stressful cockpit environments on pilot performance. The job took him on field trials around the world – Cyprus, the Persian Gulf, the

in 1982. In 1988 he transferred to Groton as Central Research's senior vice president for Clinical Research.

Among his contributions to Central Research, Saxton has overseen integration of Pfizer's clinical resources around the world, including those in Groton, New York, Japan and Europe, putting the company in a much better position to compete. He has advanced the R2D2 process, in which experts plan Phase III trials in order to opti-

Craig A. P. D. Saxton

Craig Allan Paul Dance Saxton (the priest who christened him threw in a saint's name, Paul, and his mother insisted on her maiden name of Dance) grew up in Yorkshire near the city of Leeds, where he became a lifelong golf addict at the tender age of 12.

Being a physician, however, was all he ever seriously considered as a profession. He took his Bachelor of Science in Anatomy at Leeds University in 1962 and completed his Doctorate in Medicine there three years later. "Apart from scholastic activities, I played a lot of bridge," he recalls. "I made many good friends and supported the local brewery." He was also on the university golf

Maldive Islands, Singapore, Germany and Hong Kong.

As a research fellow, he had enjoyed early clinical exploration of new drugs and through that work, an association with several pharmaceutical companies. So, when an old friend got a position with Pfizer's European Central Research headquarters, Saxton decided to join. He started as a medical advisor working on cardiovascular drugs, which were Sandwich's main output at the time. In 1981 he moved to New York as senior associate medical director for Pfizer's International Division, becoming vice president and medical director of the division

mize new products. He has maximized the potential of several new products by working to assure development of additional indications and dosage forms. Finally, Saxton has introduced a prioritization process in which each department contributes data in order to rank development candidates, leading to a systematic method for making rational portfolio decisions. He and John Niblack established the Early Clinical Research Groups in Groton and Sandwich in 1988.

Since coming to the United States, Saxton has had a chance to take up golf again (he still has a handicap of seven or eight). Every weekend in summer, he plays with other low handicappers. He looks forward to golfing vacations in Scotland, where he plays with old friends from Pfizer. "The older I get, the more I love it," he says. "It's one of the very few games you can play from the moment you start walking until the day you stop walking!"

He and his wife Pietrina, whom he met at Pfizer, spend winter vacations over Christmas and New Year's skiing in the Rockies or Europe. Both are opera fans, attending performances whenever they can and listening to the music when they can't. Of his three children from his previous marriage, the eldest, a daughter, recently graduated from medical school at Cornell to start her residency in pediatrics at Columbia and presented him with his first grandson; one son runs a business in Boulder, Colorado, and the other is soon to start postgraduate studies in environmental policy at Duke University.

In 1993, Craig Saxton was appointed executive vice president of Central Research, in which role he is responsible for coordinating the development of drugs that come out of the Discovery pipeline. "I've done several jobs in my time with Pfizer," he says in retrospect. "And I've never been anything other than excited and challenged by them."

Familiar from his early years with the demands of the medical profession, Craig Saxton was just the man Central Research needed to help refine the development process in order to meet the current challenges of new drug development. His current position as executive vice president of Central Research allows him to do just that.

modern electron microscope that, projected on a screen, shows vividly the 100 million crawling bacteria in a few drops of saliva.

Another critical point at which Pfizer intervenes is between junior and senior years of college, when many

Pamela Ann Mooney, Ohio State University   *Faculty Mentor: Professor Paquette*

Synthesis of Oxygen-Containing Ionophores of Unusual Structural Type

Professor E. J. Corey of Harvard, a Nobel laureate, left, and George Milne, president of Central Research, pause to view a poster presentation of a student fellow from Ohio State University.

students are considering whether or not to go on to graduate school in the sciences. For the past six years, Central Research has sponsored undergraduate summer research fellowships in chemistry, biology and pharmacy, awarding some 50 students $5,000 each to pursue a research project on campus under the eye of a faculty advisor. About 30 of the fellowships go to students in New England area colleges where Pfizer recruits; the balance go to students at nationally known, major research universities like Cal Tech, Stanford, Harvard and MIT. In the fall, after the completion of their projects, award re-

cipients and their faculty advisors are invited to Central Research headquarters in Groton to show off the results of their research and take a tour of the laboratories.

The newest program, begun in the fall of 1993, is an attempt to upgrade the teaching of freshman college chemistry and biology, which needs improvement at many colleges in order to offset the well-documented atrophy of student interest at this stage of the study of science and math. The Pfizer Foundation has underwritten grants of $10,000 to $20,000 to 15 colleges in New England to support curriculum development aimed at more imaginative approaches that will get more students excited about the subjects.

Also initiated in 1993 was a program to support research in synthetic organic chemistry, which plays a pivotal role in drug discovery yet has shown signs of waning in academia. Senior faculty grants of $20,000 a year, renewable for two additional years, were awarded to five distinguished scientists, including Nobel Laureate E. J. Corey and David Evans of Harvard, Samuel Danishefsky of Yale, Clayton Heathcock of the University of California at Berkeley and Barry Trost of Stanford. New-faculty grants of $25,000 a year, renewable for three additional years, were awarded to Eric Jacobsen of the University of Illinois, Andrew Myers of the California Institute of Technology and Scott Rychnovsky of the University of Minnesota.

Central Research and its People

In addition to involvement in problems of the outside world, Pfizer's "soul" is also an internal affair. That, in fact, is what makes Pfizer the remarkable company it is – and that makes people *want* to work there.

First of all, when Pfizer recruits, it goes for the best. "Our secret weapon has always been that we hire the best people, and keep them by treating them right," says William Steere, Pfizer's CEO. The company also makes special efforts to teach new recruits what the old

hands have learned over the years, instead of throwing them in and ignoring them.

To give its scientists a sense of recognition and advancement, Central Research established a "scientific ladder" that they can climb. It begins with assistant scientist and progresses upwards through associate scientist, scientist, research scientist and senior research scientist, these promotions are reviewed by a committee consisting largely of their peers. Above these levels, reviewed by another committee, are senior research

P fizer Central Research continues to attract new generations of talented research scientists with a supportive atmosphere that rewards innovation and leadership.

investigator, equivalent to a project leader on the management ladder; principal research investigator, equivalent to a manager; research advisor, equivalent to an assistant director; and, finally, senior research fellow, equivalent to

Kenneth Koe, left, and Willard Welch believe that the visionary approach that is such a part of the Central Research culture is conducive to the discovery of widely successful drugs. The result of their concerted effort, Zoloft, is one of the most successful antidepressant agents available today.

a director. The latter position is reserved for those individuals whose knowledge and influence are exceptional among a group of distinguished peers and whose long-term accomplishments have contributed significantly toward meeting corporate objectives.

What attracts people to the company and motivates them to stay is the stimulating and rewarding environment Pfizer has to offer.

Pfizer is goal-oriented, with its feet on the ground. It makes sure there are end products that will keep it going. To do so, it spares no expense. Says Willard Welch, one of the inventors of Zoloft: "This company has resources to do organic synthesis and biological research equal to, or better than, any university anywhere, and that includes Yale, Harvard, Stanford, Oxford and Cambridge."

Pfizer gives employees freedom to do their own research; it outlines the objective, but it is up to the individual as to how to get there. Says Alan Ganong, a chemist at Groton: "They expect you to define your own role, and that's kind of neat." Says Willard Welch: "Pfizer is a lot more future-oriented than most places. We'll try to attack a problem that doesn't seem to have a solution. We'll try an approach that's never been tried before."

At Pfizer, the lines of communications are always open. "I was impressed that during my first three years I had met Jack Powers, Ed Pratt and Gerry Laubach and had shaken hands with them at my desk – they had taken the trouble to come and meet scientists in the labs," says Mike Sewell of Sandwich. "One of the most refreshing things about Pfizer is your ability to have very close communication with senior management," says Steve Ryder of Groton. "That access is one of the company's greatest strengths."

Pfizer management is young – and home-grown. "We have an unusual stability of leadership," says John Niblack. "We have an unbroken chain of four generations of heads of Research who have all been developed internally – Laubach, Bloom, Niblack, Milne. We've maintained a history, a memory, and we have learned from our past mistakes. If you constantly bring in top management from outside, there is no institutional memory, and they bring in their own associates. That is disruptive; the organization takes a long time to settle back down after that kind of a culture shock. This has happened in many other pharmaceuti-

Fun times are what make the people who work at Central Research more friends and teammates than coworkers. Above, the Discovery Management Committee (DMC) takes a "Break from Business" in Nantucket. Below, the Document Preparation Department in Groton shows its Halloween spirit.

cal companies – at Merck, SmithKline, Bristol-Myers and Upjohn. It has not happened at Pfizer, and I view that as a great strength."

Pfizer strives for excellence in everything it does. "We are constantly stimulated, coaxed and cajoled to perform at our best every day," says Dilip Mehta of Groton. "We don't take no for an answer. We try to solve problems, then go back to management and say, 'Look, this is the way we think we should do it,' and management asks some questions and then supports us. It's a company that isn't afraid to try different things." Says Fred Ziegler, vice president for employee resources: "Whatever the objective is, there is an overriding desire to do it right – not to just be expedient or do things second class, but to be first rate."

At Pfizer, everyone has a say. "Even people who sweep the floors in the evening feel like they are valued contributors," says Jim Matthew, assistant director of the Protein Science and Molecular Structure Group at

A job at Central Research is definitely more than just a job. Employees work hard both inside and outside the office. Extraordinary individual and team effort is expressed and rewarded at events like the Pfizer triathlon, background. Opposite, Pfizer employees help build a playground in New London, Connecticut, as part of the United Way's Day of Caring.

Groton. "If they see something that ought to be changed, someone will listen and value their opinion."

Pfizer celebrates the individual and the group. When Pfizer files a New Drug Application, Central Research throws a divisionwide party in the cafeteria or has a cookout in a tent outside. When a new drug is approved for launch, the stops are pulled out – a real celebration with lots of food, balloons, posters, T-shirts, souvenirs, pictures of the celebrants and acknowledgment of the principal players in the development of the drug. There are also constant smaller celebrations. Says Jeff Stritar: "The thing that has impressed me is that *all*

of the people who retire from Pfizer have retirement parties. I don't remember a single retirement party when I worked at other pharmaceutical companies. The atmosphere there was quite different; people frequently came and went; there seemed to be no hesitation to move people out at any time in their career. Pfizer is a company that cares about its employees and vice versa. People like working here. They feel that they're part of the show."

Individuals in Central Research are recognized for their outstanding achievements. Each year about 1 percent of the Central Research employees from all sites and at all job levels are singled out for their extraordinary contributions and accomplishments by the awarding of Central Research Achievement Awards. The award recognizes a strong employee performance that has been marked by a specific accomplishment worthy of special notice. Part of the selection criteria involves the degree to which an employee has demonstrated initiative that led to a specific achievement above normal performance expectations. The awards have been granted each year since 1989. Each awardee receives a commemorative sculpture (commissioned specifically for this purpose),

Barry Bloom and many of the executive assistants of the Groton office pose outside the front entrance of the building, on the occasion of his retirement, below. Pfizer Central Research values all of the men and women who work there. The company takes every opportunity to reward and show appreciation for its employees, including the creation of a walking trail, left, for relaxing breaks for employees at the Groton campus.

Central Research celebrates team effort and individual performance as a part of that team. The Central Research Achievement Awards, instituted in 1989, recognize individuals who have made a contribution to the company far beyond what was required. Pictured above are many of the 1995 Achievement Award honorees from Groton, right, and Sandwich. Each of them receives a hand sculpted award, left. Below, John Niblack, Bill Steere and George Milne, from left to right, congratulate James Retsema, center, on his Achievement Award in 1992.

which is presented at a special ceremony attended by senior management. Forty Central Research employees worldwide were identified in 1995, many having been nominated by their peers. Says George Milne, "Although we couldn't operate without teams, our performance depends ultimately on personal initiative, on people who go out and raise the standards for teams and for the organization as a whole."

Central Research celebrates its successes. Here, from left to right, Al Weissman, Kenneth Koe, Willard Welch and Chuck Harbert enjoy a celebration party marking the filing of Zoloft's NDA in 1988.

At Pfizer, there is a warm, collegial atmosphere. "Have you heard the expression 'the Pfizer family?' It's about as corny as you can get for a company, especially one with 40,000 employees. But it's true," said Jack Powers, former CEO. "There's a feeling of mutual re-

spect, of enthusiasm for what you're doing," says Alan Proctor. "People have a high regard for each other; there isn't much petty territorialism. Everyone's in this together; everyone's struggling to be efficient, to get the job done." Says Joe Lombardino: "I have been with Pfizer for 38 years and have watched the company and the Research Division transformed from a small player in 1957 to a world-class operation today. Yet through all the changes, I still feel very much a part of the Pfizer family."

Pfizer is stable. "Stability derived from financial success allows people to focus sharply on what they need to do without worrying about their job security," says Frank Sciavolino. "Some friends of mine at other drug companies are worried about whether they're going to have a job next week." Pfizer's moral standards are second to none. "What makes Pfizer different is that we have a culture that is highly ethical and highly motivated," says former CEO Ed Pratt. "We've also tried to make it a fun place in which to work."

Add to all that a superb location for Central Research headquarters in Groton. Southeastern Connecticut combines the advantages of living in small-town, coastal New England with accessibility to major metropolitan areas, varied recreation, a reasonable cost of living and the educational opportunities of nearby Connecticut College, Wesleyan, Yale and Brown. (As part of its efforts to retain and develop its scientific talent, Pfizer recently concluded an arrangement with the latter university to offer a Masters in Science curriculum — paid for by the company — at the Central Research campus.)

When all is said and done, however, the bottom line is the discovery of new drugs.

"Most people who go into science, despite their gruff, analytical style, are essentially romantics," says George Milne. "Finding a medicine that makes a difference in somebody's life is really all that counts."

"As a scientist, I want to do good science," says Ken Richardson. "But most of all I want to discover a drug that will save people's lives. We're not trying to astonish the world by how many papers we publish. We want to astonish the world, and worry our competitors, by how many drugs we put on the market – not 'me-too' medicines, but really effective, innovative drugs."

Says Peter Ringrose: "What distinguishes Pfizer from its competitors is a commitment, an eagerness, a hunger to discover new drugs to treat disease. When Diflucan went into the first patients, we got letters saying things like, 'Without your drug my daughter would have died.'

"That makes it all worthwhile. That's the reward that keeps me on the job."

On a sunny day outside the Groton headquarters building, a member of the Central Research team sits and enjoys the atmosphere. This relaxed environment allows employees the freedom to seek solutions to problems that another company might consider out of reach.

Electron Microscopy

Electrophysiology

Employee Health

Employee Resources

Endocrinology

Entomology

Environmental Science

Enzymology

Facilities Maintenance

Fermentation Research

Finance

A Spectrum of Jobs

From analytical chemists to X-ray spectroscopists, it takes all kinds of specialists to run Central Research. Each plays a vital role in the long, complex pharmaceutical R&D process. The incredible diversity of professions is reflected in a representative listing of disciplines within the division:

Administrative Support

Analytical Chemistry

Animal Health

Anti-infective Disease

Bacteriology

Behavioral Science

Biochemistry

Biology

Biometrics

Cardiology

Cardiovascular Science

Cell Biology

Chemical Engineering

Chemistry

Clinical Research

Communication

Computational Chemistry

Computer Science

Controlled Release

Cytogenetics

Development Planning

DNA Sequencing

Diabetology

Document Preparation

Dosage Form Development

Drug Absorption

Drug Degradation

Drug Delivery

Electrical Engineering

Food Technology

Formulation Development

Gastroenterology

Graphic Design

Histomorphometry

Immunology

Information Technology

Intestinal Permeability

Law

Library Science

Marine Biology

Mass Spectroscopy

Mechanical Engineering

Medicinal Chemistry

Medicine

Metabolism

Microbiology

Molecular Biology

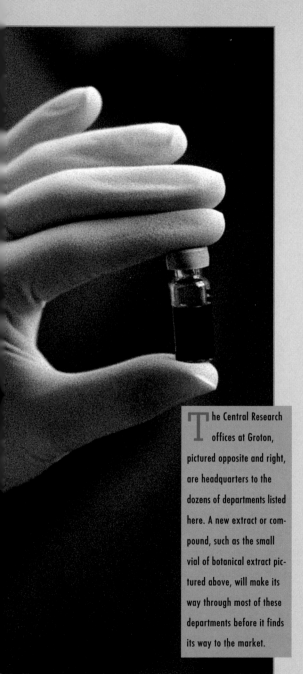

Molecular Genetics

Molecular Models

Natural Products

Neurobiology

Neurochemistry

Neurology

Neurophysiology

NMR Spectroscopy

Nursing

Nutrition

Obesity Research

Oncology

Organic Chemistry

Packaging

Parasitology

Pathology

Peptide Chemistry

Pharmacokinetics

Pharmacology

Photochemistry

Physical Chemistry

Physiology

Phytochemistry

Planning

Powder Flow Research

Process Development

Project Management

Protein Chemistry

Psychiatry

Psychobiology

Psychology

Public Relations

Pulmonary Physiology

Radiochemistry

Research Planning

Rheumatology

Robotics

Spectroscopy

Statistics

Sterile Manufacturing

Tabletting

Taxonomy

Technical Information

Toxicology

Transdermal Drug Delivery

Veterinary Science

Virology

X-ray Spectroscopy

The Central Research offices at Groton, pictured opposite and right, are headquarters to the dozens of departments listed here. A new extract or compound, such as the small vial of botanical extract pictured above, will make its way through most of these departments before it finds its way to the market.

Pfizer

10

Gazing into a microscope, Melissa Tassinari of Reproductive Toxicology in Groton may be gazing into the future of Pfizer. The importance Pfizer places on research and development today will translate into improved quality of life for the people of tomorrow. Whatever changes may take place in health-related fields over the next few years will not change the fact that quality pharmaceutical products are the best, most cost-effective, treatments that health-care professionals can give their patients.

CHAPTER TEN
Looking to the Future

Where does Pfizer Inc want to go? How does Pfizer Central Research plan to change and evolve to meet the challenges of an ever-changing health-care environment in the U.S. and around the world? These difficult questions are being addressed in a variety of ways.

Educational Programs for Government, Patients and the Public

Getting government and the public to understand what the company does and why, is one of the biggest challenges facing Pfizer and the rest of the industry. To underline how bad the situation is, a recent *Wall Street Journal* / NBC News poll found that only 18 percent of the American public had a positive view of the pharmaceutical industry. In an attempt to correct this low public opinion, Pfizer makes these factual points in its advertising and before various interest groups:

The marketplace for new drugs may be getting tougher and the process of drug discovery more complex, but the tools that Central Research uses in the discovery process are becoming much more advanced. This Sandwich scientist can depict and analyze the molecular structure of various chemicals on a computer screen, making the design process more accurate and much faster.

• Pharmaceuticals, the first line of medical treatment, account for only 7 percent of the U.S. bill for health care. They are a bargain, with the potential to generate even more impressive cost savings to the entire health-care system. For example, a year's supply of ulcer medication costs about $1,000; the surgery it replaces costs 25 times that amount. Treating heart disease with a calcium channel blocker costs about $600 a year; in many cases, this drug eliminates the need for highly invasive heart bypass surgery costing $40,000 or more.

• The results of the industry's massive investment in R&D are evident: of the 100 most-prescribed drugs in the U.S., 99 were discovered, developed and patented by private industry. U.S. pharmaceutical companies account

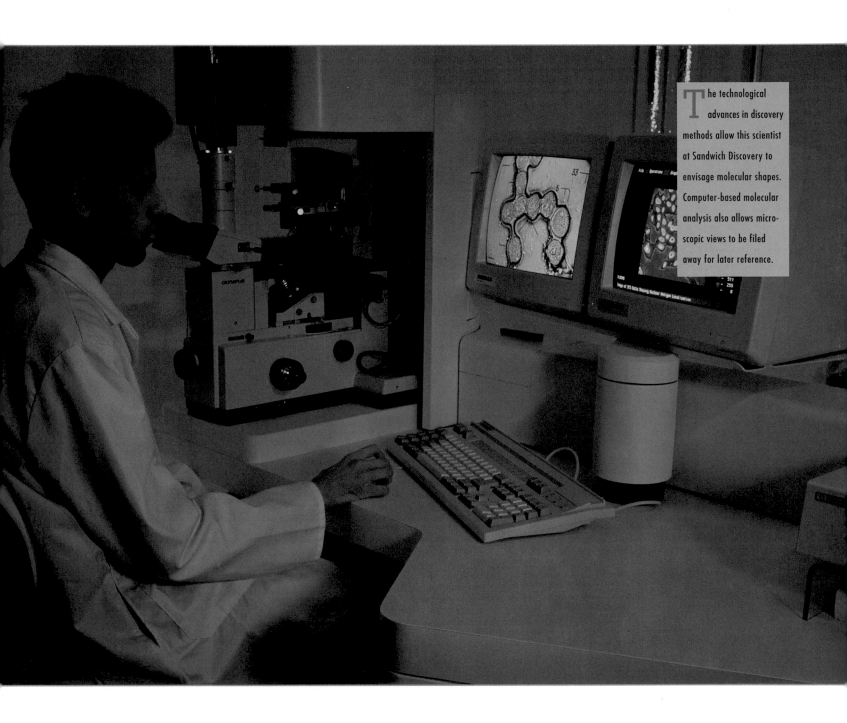

The technological advances in discovery methods allow this scientist at Sandwich Discovery to envisage molecular shapes. Computer-based molecular analysis also allows microscopic views to be filed away for later reference.

for half of all new drugs introduced world-wide, more than·three times the number from any other country.

• Prices of drugs are lower in the United States than they are in many other countries. The average American works only two-thirds as many hours to pay his annual drug bill as does his German, French or Japanese counterpart.

• Clearly a major problem in drug treatments is patient noncompliance. A recent drug industry report indicates that Americans fail to take their medicine as prescribed half the time. Some patients skip doses or stop taking their medication early; others don't even get their prescriptions filled. Such lapses cost an estimated $100 billion in added medical bills and lost productivity. Pfizer's research is addressing this problem by producing drugs whose dosing regimen is more accommodating of patients' schedules.

The Changing Marketplace for Pharmaceuticals

"We're experiencing truly dramatic marketplace changes" says Karen Katen, president, U.S. Pharmaceuticals Group (USPG). "Ten years ago the U.S. population received its primary health care mainly on a fee-for-ser-

Karen Katen, president of Pfizer's U.S. Pharmaceuticals Group, understands well America's pharmaceutical industry. Her background in marketing has helped prepare her for the rapidly changing health-care environment and convinced her that quality products that offer patients improved care at a good value are in demand, now more than ever.

vice basis. Each doctor's visit, surgical procedure, prescription medication, etc., was an independent event, with little or no coordination. Now, increasingly large and sophisticated managed care organizations are exerting considerable control over care delivery. This revolution in how health care is delivered and paid for has affected virtually every player in the marketplace – and it's far from over.

"Interestingly, we are seeing as much fragmentation as we are consolidation. In California, for example, there is movement away from highly restrictive staff-model HMOs. At the same time, large physician practice groups are emerging that are bypassing managed care organizations by directly contracting with employers to provide care. It's very hard to say at this point exactly where the marketplace is headed."

This dynamic operating environment has led to an expansion in the number and type of customers Pfizer must serve. In the past, these have included solo practice physicians, hospitals and pharmacists. While these traditional customers are still critically important, Pfizer must also serve a variety of new customer groups that have different needs. In addition to managed care organizations, these include physician practice groups, employers and consumers.

Says Katen, "As a result of the rise of managed care and other new customer groups, the very definition of our product is evolving. In addition to representing significant advances in efficacy, safety and convenience – relative to existing therapies – successful new products must increasingly incorporate value components such as medical outcomes, pharmacoeconomics, provider and patient educational materials, quality-of-life assessments and, ultimately, improved patient outcome."

"Assuring that we bring products to market that our customers truly value will require unprecedented cooperation and teamwork between Central Research and the operating divisions," says Edward Bessey, former vice chairman, Pfizer Inc, now retired.

"You need to get the best input you can into the development process at a very early stage – when a product is just entering Phase II trials – so that you can begin to shape your development plan in a way that is

Hank McKinnell, executive vice president of Pfizer Inc, is responsible for the U.S. Pharmaceuticals business, the worldwide Consumer Healthcare business and the company's financial functions. Hank believes that the key to Pfizer's future success in all its businesses will be innovation and a spirit of continuous improvement.

most likely going to give your product the differentiation and value you'd like to have. This must include medical and economic outcomes studies. Even though the product might be six or eight years from launch, you've got to anticipate as best you can what the marketplace is going to look like from a medical and competitive point of view and design your development programs accordingly. And that's tough."

Katen agrees: "We must work more closely with Central Research than ever before. This is especially true because of the expanding scope of what our products must include to be viable in the marketplace."

Improving patient outcomes – the quality of care – is becoming a growing focus for many managed care organizations. This issue is being pursued by both consumers and employers who are concerned that quality could be eroded by a cost-driven approach. Once managed care organizations have squeezed costs out of the system, Katen believes, the basis of competition will likely shift to improving quality of care. The more enlightened provider organizations realize this and are beginning to move in that di-

The sophistication of the Nagoya facility has greatly increased since the early 1970s. Noako Lio, left, uses special enclosed equipment to handle a compound that is oxygen sensitive. The screening of compounds at Nagoya is an integral part of the Central Research worldwide team.

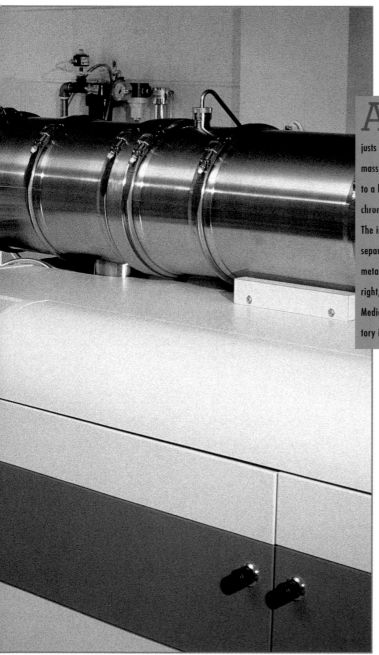

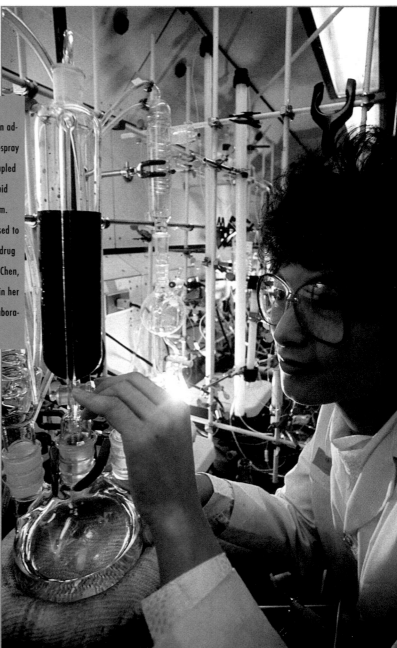

At left, Cornelia Buser of Groton adjusts settings of an ion-spray mass spectrometer coupled to a high-pressure liquid chromatography system. The instruments are used to separate and identify drug metabolites. Yuhpyng Chen, right, runs a reaction in her Medicinal Chemistry laboratory in Groton.

rection. Consumer and employer activism will play a key role in furthering this process and, as a result, shaping the evolution of the health-care marketplace.

"We are working with a wide variety of provider organizations to help them demonstrably improve the quality of care they provide. Not only do we offer cost-effective, high-quality medicines, but we have also developed a variety of sophisticated disease management programs. In this sense, Pfizer is truly part of the cure because we are helping our managed care customers be better at what they do and enhancing the lives of patients at the same time."

Katen concludes, "Pfizer's future success will be dependent on our ability to continue to respond to the changing marketplace by having the appropriate products, education and information approach and an organization that will allow us to meet changing customer needs, be quickly responsive and flexible, and continuously improve our efficiency and effectiveness."

Bob Neimeth, president of the International Pharmaceuticals Group (IPG), points out that: "In the state-subsidized system of Western Europe and Japan,

Robert Neimeth, as president of Pfizer's International Pharmaceuticals Group, is responsible for marketing Pfizer's products in foreign markets. The varied health care systems throughout the world present a difficult challenge for Pfizer's overseas ventures and require Central Research to develop new drugs that offer a new standard of care and are of unique value to all patients.

the cost containment environment has made these conditions prevalent for decades. For instance, restrictive lists, price control, reference pricing and global budgets are techniques well in evidence overseas, and these place pressure on our company to provide truly the most innovative, differentiable medicines.

"Throughout the world, in the nationally subsidized systems, Europe, Japan and the developing world, our medicines must also provide value. But we also believe our medicines can provide enormous value to all people around the globe, regardless of the particular country's political and economic state of development. Our exciting new venture in Vietnam is an excellent example, and our organization in China, now almost a decade old, with a first-class, state-of-the-art pharmaceutical plant, is another." Indeed, Robert Neimeth says: "Our hallmark has been a global position for the long term which is well illustrated by our longstanding and successful positions in North America, Latin America, Africa, the Middle East and Asia, in addition to all of Europe – Western and Eastern."

New Management Procedures

It was to address urgent matters arising from the rapidly changing pharmaceutical business environment that the Pharmaceutical Steering Committee (PSC) was formed at Pfizer. Early in 1993, about 30 key people from Pfizer — including representatives from Central Research, U.S. Pharmaceuticals, International Pharmaceuticals, Licensing, and Corporate Planning — met off-site. This group deliberated for three days and then formed a steering committee to implement means for solving specific problems. George Milne of Central

Research was the first to hold the position of chairman of the Pharmaceutical Steering Committee, a position that rotates on a yearly basis, with chairpersons having included Karen Katen of USPG and Brian Barrett of IPG.

"We tried to put on the table what the real issues were, the challenges for our worldwide business in the foreseeable future," says Bessey. "This was the first time that all the elements had really gotten together and talked."

Another product of the off-site meeting, which has become an annual event, was the formation of the Global Pharmaceutical Management Team (GPMT). It

Number of Candidates

Phase III NCE Candidates In the Pfizer Pipeline, 1970-1995

The sharply increased number of late-stage clinical candidates required new processes and management techniques.

	1970	1975	1980	1985	1990	1995*
16						
14						Dofetilide
						Ziprasidone
12						Trovafloxacin
						Droloxifene
10						E-2020
						E-5
8						D-99
						Tandospirone
						Sildenafil
6						Voriconazole
						Candoxatril
4				Sorbinil		Zopolrestat
			Trimazosin	Doxazosin		CP-93,393
2			Sulprostone	Sertraline	Azithromycin	Darifenacin IBS/UU
	Prazosin	Feldene	Pirbuterol	Amlodipine	Tenidap	Eletriptan
0	Tinidazole	Tolamolol	Levonantradol	Unasyn	Candoxatril	

* Projected for 1995 including late phase candidates

consists of the heads of the major pharmaceutical groups at Pfizer: the International Pharmaceuticals Group, the U.S. Pharmaceuticals Group and Central Research. These senior managers meet regularly to set the worldwide strategy and facilitate the implementation of tactics for Pfizer's global pharmaceutical business.

Pfizer is making changes which can bring even better quality health care to patients. George Milne puts it this way: "Historically, our business has been defined by many in terms of the chemicals that we put into pills. In fact, our broader and more appropriate mission is health, wellness. If a patient has diabetes or hypertension, the treatment isn't just the pill they take, it's whether or not they're eating properly, whether or not they're reducing stress. In today's fragmented health-care system, none of this has been brought together in a holistic view. This is the power of rethinking our role as leaders in disease management."

However, this type of change is not accomplished without overcoming hurdles. Says Bill Steere, "We're seeing seismic shifts in the health-care marketplace. Worldwide trends toward cost containment and health-care reform exert constant pressure on pricing, and we're experiencing a public policy climate in which government and regulatory involvement in every step of our business is likely to intensify. The pharmaceutical

A Central Research scientist checks readings on a nuclear magnetic resonance (NMR) imager to help identify the specific structure of a newly synthesized compound. The sophisticated technology that Central Research has built into the process of drug discovery helps ensure that drugs coming out of the pipeline today are specific to the medical problems they are meant to treat.

industry is becoming an ever more costly and demanding arena in which to compete, with substantial penalties for those who do poorly. But it's also an industry with excellent rewards for those who do well."

Pfizer Central Research — Changing to Meet the Challenges

Despite the obvious success of Pfizer Central Research, it is not allowing itself to rest on its laurels. The nature of the pharmaceutical business is changing so rapidly that there is an urgent need to continually re-examine the way research does its business in order to maximize efficiency and to ensure success in the future. And a key to this success is Central Research's belief in

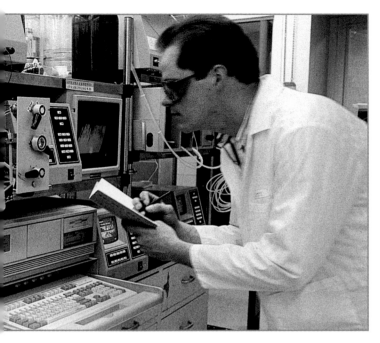

quality, as evidenced in its continual quest for new ways to do everything it does even better. An additional challenge, though a welcome one, is the increased workload resulting form Pfizer's development pipeline being fuller that ever before.

Since 1994, each of the key phases in the R&D process of pharmaceutical research has been carefully analyzed by teams of Pfizer scientists who are closest to the action. From the initial idea all the way to final regulatory approval, every process and procedure is being examined and questioned. Does this add value? Can this be done smarter, better, faster and for less? How can awareness of the ever-changing needs of the medical

community and marketplace help enhance the quality of our new medicines?

"At Central Research sites around the world, task forces of our most talented people – from all levels and across all functions – are engaged in coordinated efforts," says George Milne, "building more quality and value into R&D." Examples of some of the many areas of analysis include idea generation, strategic thinking, future analyses, design and management of candidate portfolios, globalization and drug development efficiency.

To date, many procedures have been improved in this ongoing process of self-analysis. Re-engineering the drug discovery process has involved the use of automation and high-speed technologies which have greatly streamlined the entire process. John LaMattina, vice president, U.S. Discovery Operations, with obvious pride says, "Historically, going from an idea to a clinical candidate at Pfizer involved upwards of 50 staff-years of effort. In many cases, this now can be accomplished in 15-20 staff-years. As a result, Discovery can operate a higher number of programs simultaneously, thereby broadening the number of novel approaches to any given therapeutic target."

The Research Division's operational units of Discovery, Exploratory Development and Full Development now function in an increasingly seamless manner. Gone are the old "hand-offs" of product and relinquishing of re-

The Pharmaceutical Steering Committee, established in 1993, is helping Central Research focus its efforts by providing a channel of communication between Pfizer's three main divisions: International Pharmaceuticals, U.S. Pharmaceuticals and Central Research. On the right, PSC members from U.S. Pharmaceuticals — left to right: Peter Brandt, Chuck Dombeck, Karen Katen and Fred Telling — along with George Milne, 1993 chair of the committee, listen to suggestions.

sponsibility at artificial transfer points in the pipeline. Today people in scientific and management teams share responsibility for and help support a candidate throughout its lifetime in the R&D process. The experts closest to the drug candidate make the decisions, and the extent of their involvement and motivation has never been higher.

Craig Saxton guided the worldwide development and clinical resources to support a single global strategy and plan. Furthermore, extension of the clinical theater of operations from multiple sites in Europe, to the Middle East, Africa, India, Latin America and Australia allows access to a wider patient population and diverse diseases. It also enables added clinical studies at reduced cost.

According to Bob Neimeth, a critical element in this global research framework is an adequate structure for intellectual property (IP) – full product patent rights as well as trademark protection. In country after country, we have seen better and better IP protection. Canada, China, South Korea, Russia, Bulgaria, Taiwan and Eastern Europe are examples of the many countries which

At left, members of the PSC from various departments — left to right: Leigh Stone of International Pharmaceuticals, Dan O'Shea from Central Research and Dick Fulmer of Licensing and Development — brainstorm about new directions. It will be this type of interdepartmental collaboration that will help Pfizer get the maximum return on its investment in research and bring the most necessary and effective new drugs to markets all over the world.

in recent years have all enacted such laws protecting IP. We continue to press on in Argentina, Brazil, Turkey and India, important markets which still lack adequate patent laws. To provide a system in which innovation is rewarded, these countries must provide full product patent rights with immediate application.

Other examples of improved procedures in Central Research extend all the way through to registration. Case record forms have been improved and simplified. Clinical data can now be electronically entered into Central Research's database management systems directly at the trial site, and the new network facilitates electronic querying and resolution of issues.

The continual process of change that is vital to Central Research's success in the global pharmaceutical sector is mirrored in its worldwide Animal Health R&D. With the recent expansion of this business through the SmithKline Beecham acquisition, Central Research is more able than ever to meet the health needs of both feed and companion animals.

being transformed. Hospitals, physicians' practices and pharmaceutical companies alike are being driven towards consolidation. The health-care industry in the 1990s is ex-

Steere's answer to these pressures is to highlight the importance of new products. In his view, as he told Pfizer shareholders at a recent annual meeting, "the successful health-care companies of the future will have to be able to offer new therapies that meet unmet medical needs and enhance quality of life. Assured access alone is not enough. New products alone are not enough. To be truly successful, a company will need both."

William C. Steere, Jr.

"Our basic strategy is to innovate our way – through productive research – out of the challenges our industry faces," Chairman and Chief Executive Officer, Bill Steere, frequently tells audiences both within and outside of Pfizer.

Bill Steere joined Pfizer as a medical service representative in 1959, fresh out of Stanford University. In the years that followed, he advanced through a variety of marketing and senior management positions. In 1986, Steere was named president of Pfizer Pharmaceuticals Group. He became president and chief executive officer of Pfizer Inc in 1991 and chairman in 1992.

Steere took on leadership of Pfizer at a critical time. The health-care industry is

periencing the price competition, restructuring and pressures to consolidate that other American industries – including the high-tech companies of Silicon Valley – felt in the 1980s.

Steere is determined that Pfizer will have both access and new products. He recently told a group of two dozen of his fellow Fortune 500 CEOs, "To discover and develop new medicines and other technologies,

we at Pfizer have built one of the foremost research organizations in all of industry."

Interviewed in his New York office, Steere was eager for the visitor to grasp the connection between the company's exceptional research investments of recent years and its competitive edge. "The new realities of our industry mean we must constantly try to increase the productivity of our R&D operations. To do that, we've made and are continuing to make huge investments in facilities and equipment to provide our scientists with the tools and technologies they need: supercomputing, gene sequencing, nuclear magnetic resonance, molecular modeling and X-ray crystallography.

"But, frankly, an awful lot of it is having the right people — and listening to them," Steere added. "Our R&D executives are on all the key management committees and play a vital role in shaping company strategy. Meanwhile, great attention has been given to the structure of our research organization to help us make the most of the resources we have."

As chairman of the Pharmaceutical Manufacturers Association, Steere was the point man for the research-based pharmaceutical industry during the most recent national debate about health-care reform. He developed a keen awareness of the impor-

tance of educating the public about the work of the industry, the high-risk nature of drug research and the costs in time and money of moving a drug through the development pipeline.

As Steere recently told his fellow CEOs, "As we approach our 150th anniversary in 1999, all of us who work for Pfizer are proud of the work we do. In the end, our company succeeds because we save and improve patients' lives."

"'We're part of the cure,' is more than a slogan in Pfizer's advertisements," Steere tells the interviewer. "It's a way of life — and nowhere more so than in Pfizer research."

Chairman, President and CEO Bill Steere, along with his colleagues, has a clear vision of Pfizer's role in the future of the pharmaceutical industry, and that vision centers on a commitment to research and development that will produce new drugs of higher quality. Opposite, he is seen with John Niblack and Barry Bloom, bottom, and with executives of the Animal Health Division, top. As Steere explains, "innovative, cost-effective products are the lifeblood of Pfizer." Never forgetting the heart of the business, Steere also emphasizes that the future depends upon the commitment of the employees that are working at Pfizer today, assuring Pfizer's success in the decades to come.

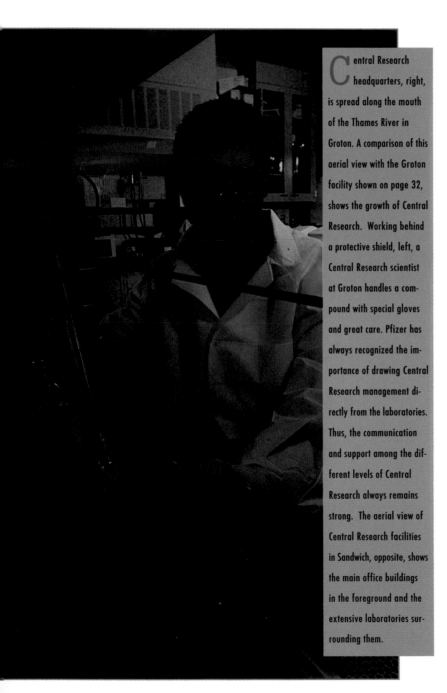

Central Research headquarters, right, is spread along the mouth of the Thames River in Groton. A comparison of this aerial view with the Groton facility shown on page 32, shows the growth of Central Research. Working behind a protective shield, left, a Central Research scientist at Groton handles a compound with special gloves and great care. Pfizer has always recognized the importance of drawing Central Research management directly from the laboratories. Thus, the communication and support among the different levels of Central Research always remains strong. The aerial view of Central Research facilities in Sandwich, opposite, shows the main office buildings in the foreground and the extensive laboratories surrounding them.

"Smarter, better, faster – these are our bywords in meeting challenge now and in the future," states George Milne.

Looking to the Future

So, what's the prognosis for Pfizer?

"I think we're going to do very well over the course of the next decade," says John Niblack. "But it's going to be a trying time for the industry, for a while at any rate, because the pharmaceutical companies have been among

the earliest targets of politicians attempting to show that they can do something to control health-care costs. What that kind of environment favors, if it favors anyone, is the people with innovative new drugs that are on the rising part of their sales and earnings growth cycle. These innovative drugs represent the most cost-effective means of treating disease.

"During the coming years, it is widely predicted that there will be more consolidation across the industry, particularly among the smaller, startup companies. Pfizer will be in a good position to take the best advantage of opportunities to enter into partnerships and collaborations with, if not outright acquire, some of the interesting small companies that are caught in this political turn of events."

Ultimately, it all boils down to what Pfizer Central Research can do for itself. Concludes Bill Steere, "We must continually increase the productivity of the R&D process, every step of the way — from the idea to the lab, in the clinical development stage, in the regulatory re-

view stage and, ultimately, in the approval stage. This is crucial to our future."

Says Barry Bloom, simply: "Research has become the battlefield in this industry. That's where the game will be won or lost."

Pfizer is poised to win.

During the 1980s and early 1990s, the company built modern research facilities around the world that are second to none. During the same period, it brought in hundreds of young, freshly trained scientists, who, with a few years of experience under their belts, are approaching

peak productivity. Pfizer scientists around the world are in close communication with one another, working on collaborative studies and interacting via video-conferencing and electronic mail for a daily exchange of scientific information. It's what makes Pfizer, as Niblack terms it, "the most nimble international research organization in the world."

During the same period, Pfizer launched six major drugs, all of which are on the up-curve of their sales growth, with years of exclusive patent life still to go. "We have also developed a very exciting portfolio of new-drug approaches across almost all the important disease areas," says John Niblack. "We are working on seven distinct new approaches to combat cardiovascular illness, five new approaches to cancer, four new approaches to Alzheimer's disease and six new approaches to diabetes. We have a pipeline of 15 new products in the late stages of development that is greater than at any time in Pfizer history. We have in our hands the drugs of 1997, 1998, 1999 and beyond. This near-term security permits us to be terrifically innovative and risk-taking in our long-range discovery tactics — a statement not all drug companies can make. No other company is in a better position to bring forth so many innovative medicines over the next 10 years.

"We are moving into the twenty-first century full speed ahead, and the best is yet to come."

Pfizer Research Milestones

1944 - Mass production of Penicillin G by deep-tank fermentation.

1950 - Introduction of Terramycin, first Pfizer antibiotic, still in use around the world. Terramycin animal-feed supplements developed as Pfizer entered the agricultural market.

1952 - Agricultural research center established in Terre Haute, Indiana.

1954 - Launch of the tetracycline antibiotic Tetracyn.

- Agrimycin, effective against costly plant diseases, is introduced.

1956 - Signemycin, first multi-spectrum antibiotic, introduced.

1957 - Viadril, first steroid anesthetic, launched.

- TAO, an oral antibiotic, introduced.

- Cancer Research Center established in Maywood, New Jersey.

- Biologics Research and Production Center opened in Terre Haute.

- Research begins in Sandwich, England.

1958 - Introduction of Diabinese, an oral hypoglycemic agent for diabetes, first major non-antibiotic product for Pfizer.

- Launch of Vistaril, a psychotherapeutic agent.

- Tran-Q introduced to promote weight gains in livestock.

1959 - Daricon and Enarax, anti-ulcer drugs, are launched.

- Banminth, an anthelmintic, is introduced.

1960 - Research is consolidated in new Groton Research Laboratories.

- Introduction of Maxipen, an acid-stable, oral penicillin.

1962 - Total synthesis of 6-methyl-6-deoxytetracycline, a major scientific achievement.

- Introduction of Renese, a once-a-day diuretic for hypertension and heart failure.

1965 - Pfizer Inc achieves $500 million dollars in sales ("5 by 5" goal is accomplished)

1966 - Rondomycin, a semisynthetic tetracycline antibiotic, is introduced.

- Fenclonine, from a fundamental research program in neurochemistry, yields a useful "orphan" drug for carcinoid tumors.

1967 - Vibramycin, a broad-spectrum, once-a-day tetracycline antibiotic, is launched.

- Navane, a potent antipsychotic agent, is introduced.

1969 - Introduction of Sinequan, an antianxiety and antidepressant drug.

1970 - Launch of Geopen, an injectable penicillin with broadened gram-negative spectrum, for treatment of serious infections.

- Introduction of Mithracin, an anti-tumor antibiotic, also useful in treatment of Paget's disease of bone.

- Launch of Lithane, for treating the manic phase of manic depression.

1971 - Launch of Mecadox, an antibacterial for swine.

- Central Research Division established, combining Pharmaceutical, Agricultural and Chemical R&D worldwide. Includes laboratories in U.S., England and France. Japanese laboratory established to search for new antibiotics.

1972 - Fasigyn, an anti-protazoal; Banminth, for parasitic infections; and Geocillin, an oral antibiotic; all launched.

- Pfizer Inc. reaches $1 billion in annual sales.

1973 - Start of Euroclin, a clinical research network in Europe.

1974 - Introduction of Emete-Con, for post-surgical vomiting.

1975 - Mansil, for schistosomiasis, is launched.

1976 - Introduction of Minipress in U.S., for control of blood pressure.

1977 - Quantrel, for treatment of whipworm, is launched.

1978 - Bacacil/Spectrobid, an oral penicillin, is developed.

1980 - Feldene for arthritis, enters major overseas markets.

   - Liquamycin, for extended treatment of infected animals, launched.

1981 - Paratect Bolus, for parasitic worms in cattle, launched.

   - Introduction of Coxistac, an anti-coccidal agent for poultry.

   - FDA approval and launch of Polydextrose, a bulking agent in food.

1982 - Feldene is introduced in the U.S.

   - Procardia, for angina, is introduced.

   - Cefobid, a broad-spectrum antibiotic, is launched.

1983 - Introduction of Trosyd, for fungal infections.

   - Exiril, for asthma, is launched.

1984 - Glucotrol, for diabetes, is launched.

1985 - Introduction of Sulperazone, an antibiotic.

1986 - Unasyn, an injectable antibiotic, is launched.

   - Rumatel, an antihelmintic for cattle, is introduced.

1989 - Launch of Procardia XL, once-a-day dosing for angina and hypertension.

1990 - Diflucan, now the world's leading antifungal drug, approved in U.S.

   - Chy-Max, a milk coagulant used in cheese-making, is launched.

1991 - Cardura, an antihypertensive, approved in U.S.

   - Litesse, an improved polydextrose, is launched.

1992 - Norvasc, for control of angina and hypertension, is launched in the U.S.

   - Introduction of Zoloft, for treatment of depression.

   - Launch of Zithromax, for respiratory and skin infections.

1993 - New Drug Application for tenidap, for treating arthritis, is the largest ever filed by Pfizer.

   - Introduction of Dairy-Lo, a fat substitute for frozen dairy desserts.

1994 - Dectomax, a broad-spectrum endectocide for the control of parasites in livestock, is launched in Brazil, Argentina and South Africa.

   - Diflucan is launched for single-dose treatment of vaginitis.

   - Pfizer acquires the Animal Health business of SmithKline Beecham.

1995 - Cardura is introduced for the treatment of benign prostate hyperplasia (BPH) in the U.S.

   - Zithromax pediatric formulation is approved in U.S.

   - Zyrtec is approved in U.S..

APPENDIX . B

Past and Present Leaders of Pfizer's Research and Development

JAMES CURRIE

Employed in Brooklyn 1917 to work in citric acid. Among the first scientists to work for Pfizer.

Left company in 1933.

RICHARD PASTERNACK

Employed 1920.

Pfizer's 1st Director of Research.

Retired in 1956.

WILBUR LAZIER

Joined Pfizer in 1948 as Director of Chemical Research.

Shared dual responsibility for synthetic chemistry and biochemistry research with Jasper Kane.

Left the company in 1953.

JASPER KANE

Joined Pfizer in 1918.

Director of Biochemical Research in 1942.

Vice President in charge of Research and Development in 1949.

Vice President for Scientific Affairs in 1960.

Shared dual responsibility for synthetic chemistry and biochemistry research with Wilbur Lazier.

Retired in 1964.

KARL BRUNINGS

Joined Pfizer in 1948 as a Research Chemist.

Later became Administrative Director of Research and Development.

Shared dual responsibility for synthetic chemistry and biochemistry research with Earnest Weber.

Left the company in 1962.

EARNEST WEBER

Joined Pfizer in 1942 as a Research Biochemist. Vice President for Research and Development in 1960. Later was Vice President for Scientific Affairs. Shared dual responsibility for synthetic chemistry and biochemistry research with Karl Brunings. Retired in 1970.

GERALD LAUBACH

Joined Pfizer in 1950. Vice President for Medicinal Products Research in 1964. Elected to Board of Directors in 1968. President of Pfizer Pharmaceuticals in 1969. Executive Vice President of Pfizer Inc in 1971. President of Pfizer Inc in 1972. Retired in 1991.

BARRY BLOOM

Joined Pfizer in 1952. President, Pfizer Central Research 1971-1990. Elected to Board of Directors in 1973. Senior Vice President for Research and Development, Pfizer Inc in 1990. Executive Vice President for Research and Developement in 1992. Retired in 1993.

JOHN NIBLACK

Joined Pfizer in 1967. Vice President, Medicinal Products Research in 1984. President, Pfizer Central Research 1990. Executive Vice President, Research and Development, Pfizer Inc 1993 to date.

GEORGE MILNE

Joined Pfizer in 1970. Vice President, R&D Operations 1985. Senior Vice President Research and Development 1988. President, Central Research 1993 to date.

Selected Organizational Charts from Central Research

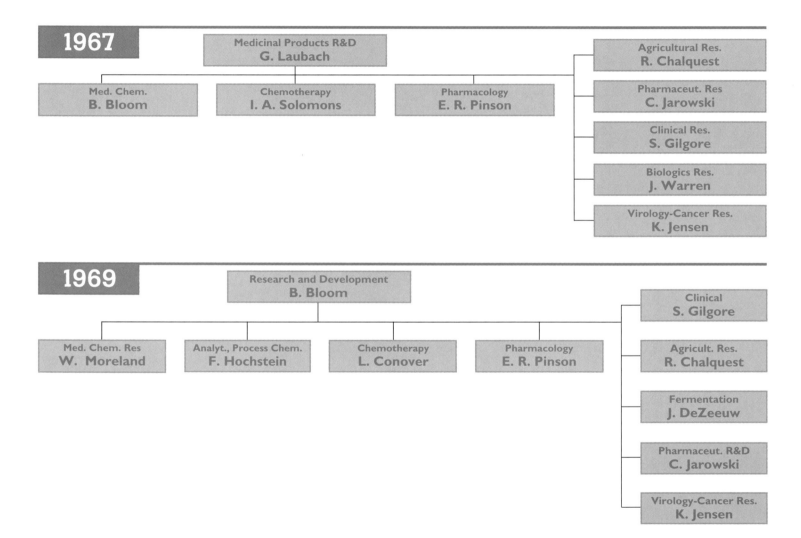

1967

Medicinal Products R&D
G. Laubach

Med. Chem.
B. Bloom

Chemotherapy
I. A. Solomons

Pharmacology
E. R. Pinson

Agricultural Res.
R. Chalquest

Pharmaceut. Res
C. Jarowski

Clinical Res.
S. Gilgore

Biologics Res.
J. Warren

Virology-Cancer Res.
K. Jensen

1969

Research and Development
B. Bloom

Med. Chem. Res
W. Moreland

Analyt., Process Chem.
F. Hochstein

Chemotherapy
L. Conover

Pharmacology
E. R. Pinson

Clinical
S. Gilgore

Agricult. Res.
R. Chalquest

Fermentation
J. DeZeeuw

Pharmaceut. R&D
C. Jarowski

Virology-Cancer Res.
K. Jensen

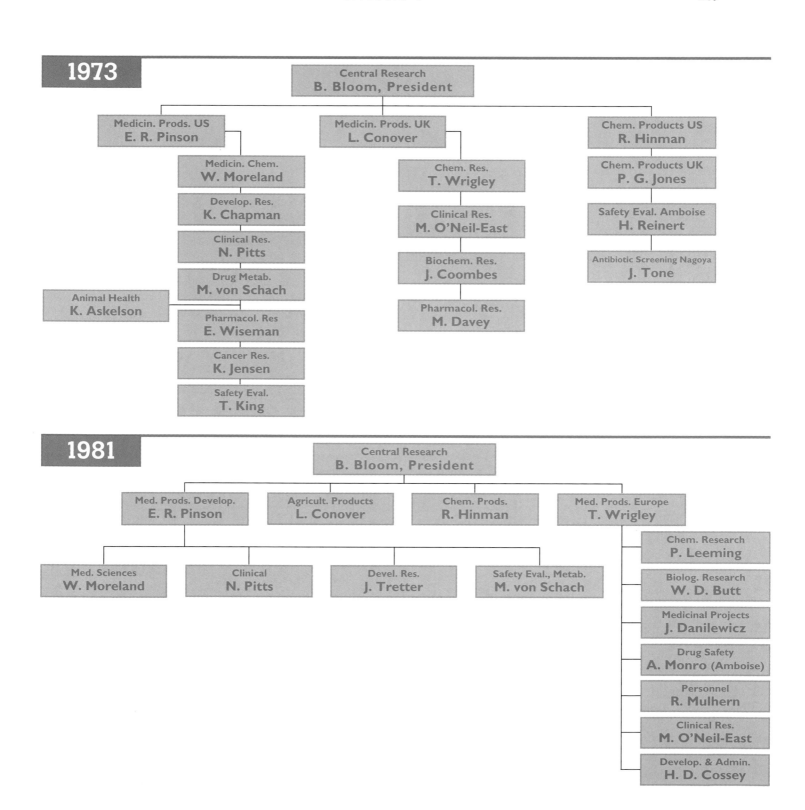

1973

Central Research
B. Bloom, President

Medicin. Prods. US
E. R. Pinson

Medicin. Chem.
W. Moreland

Develop. Res.
K. Chapman

Clinical Res.
N. Pitts

Drug Metab.
M. von Schach

Animal Health
K. Askelson

Pharmacol. Res
E. Wiseman

Cancer Res.
K. Jensen

Safety Eval.
T. King

Medicin. Prods. UK
L. Conover

Chem. Res.
T. Wrigley

Clinical Res.
M. O'Neil-East

Biochem. Res.
J. Coombes

Pharmacol. Res.
M. Davey

Chem. Products US
R. Hinman

Chem. Products UK
P. G. Jones

Safety Eval. Amboise
H. Reinert

Antibiotic Screening Nagoya
J. Tone

1981

Central Research
B. Bloom, President

Med. Prods. Develop.
E. R. Pinson

Agricult. Products
L. Conover

Chem. Prods.
R. Hinman

Med. Prods. Europe
T. Wrigley

Med. Sciences
W. Moreland

Clinical
N. Pitts

Devel. Res.
J. Tretter

Safety Eval., Metab.
M. von Schach

Chem. Research
P. Leeming

Biolog. Research
W. D. Butt

Medicinal Projects
J. Danilewicz

Drug Safety
A. Monro (Amboise)

Personnel
R. Mulhern

Clinical Res.
M. O'Neil-East

Develop. & Admin.
H. D. Cossey

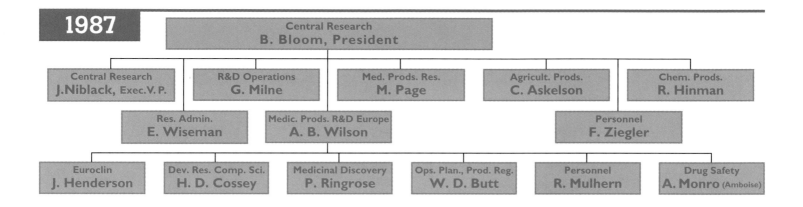

1987

Central Research
B. Bloom, President

| Central Research J.Niblack, Exec.V. P. | R&D Operations G. Milne | Med. Prods. Res. M. Page | Agricult. Prods. C. Askelson | Chem. Prods. R. Hinman |

Res. Admin.
E. Wiseman

Medic. Prods. R&D Europe
A. B. Wilson

Personnel
F. Ziegler

| Euroclin J. Henderson | Dev. Res. Comp. Sci. H. D. Cossey | Medicinal Discovery P. Ringrose | Ops. Plan., Prod. Reg. W. D. Butt | Personnel R. Mulhern | Drug Safety A. Monro (Amboise) |

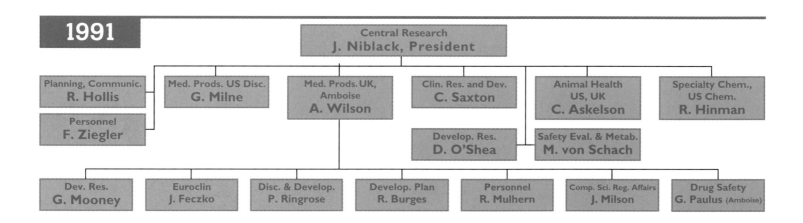

1991

Central Research
J. Niblack, President

| Planning, Communic. R. Hollis | Med. Prods. US Disc. G. Milne | Med. Prods. UK, Amboise A. Wilson | Clin. Res. and Dev. C. Saxton | Animal Health US, UK C. Askelson | Specialty Chem., US Chem. R. Hinman |

Personnel
F. Ziegler

Develop. Res.
D. O'Shea

Safety Eval. & Metab.
M. von Schach

| Dev. Res. G. Mooney | Euroclin J. Feczko | Disc. & Develop. P. Ringrose | Develop. Plan R. Burges | Personnel R. Mulhern | Comp. Sci. Reg. Affairs J. Milson | Drug Safety G. Paulus (Amboise) |

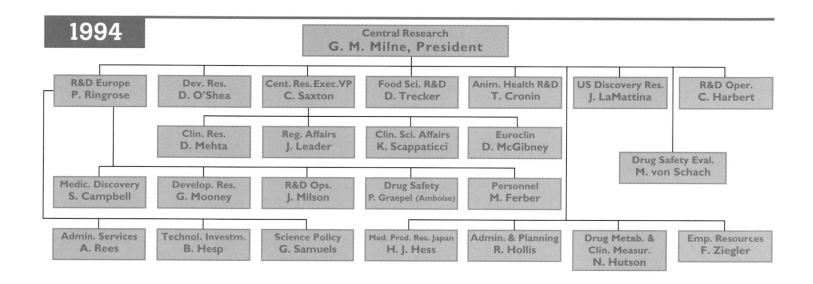

1994

Central Research
G. M. Milne, President

- R&D Europe — P. Ringrose
- Dev. Res. — D. O'Shea
- Cent. Res. Exec. VP — C. Saxton
- Food Sci. R&D — D. Trecker
- Anim. Health R&D — T. Cronin
- US Discovery Res. — J. LaMattina
- R&D Oper. — C. Harbert

- Clin. Res. — D. Mehta
- Reg. Affairs — J. Leader
- Clin. Sci. Affairs — K. Scappaticci
- Euroclin — D. McGibney

- Drug Safety Eval. — M. von Schach

- Medic. Discovery — S. Campbell
- Develop. Res. — G. Mooney
- R&D Ops. — J. Milson
- Drug Safety — P. Graepel (Amboise)
- Personnel — M. Ferber

- Admin. Services — A. Rees
- Technol. Investm. — B. Hesp
- Science Policy — G. Samuels
- Med. Prod. Res. Japan — H. J. Hess
- Admin. & Planning — R. Hollis
- Drug Metab. & Clin. Measur. — N. Hutson
- Emp. Resources — F. Ziegler

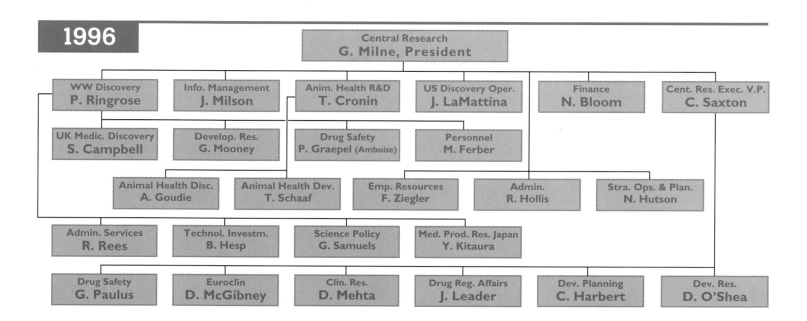

1996

Central Research
G. Milne, President

- WW Discovery — P. Ringrose
- Info. Management — J. Milson
- Anim. Health R&D — T. Cronin
- US Discovery Oper. — J. LaMattina
- Finance — N. Bloom
- Cent. Res. Exec. V.P. — C. Saxton

- UK Medic. Discovery — S. Campbell
- Develop. Res. — G. Mooney
- Drug Safety — P. Graepel (Amboise)
- Personnel — M. Ferber

- Animal Health Disc. — A. Goudie
- Animal Health Dev. — T. Schaaf
- Emp. Resources — F. Ziegler
- Admin. — R. Hollis
- Stra. Ops. & Plan. — N. Hutson

- Admin. Services — R. Rees
- Technol. Investm. — B. Hesp
- Science Policy — G. Samuels
- Med. Prod. Res. Japan — Y. Kitaura

- Drug Safety — G. Paulus
- Euroclin — D. McGibney
- Clin. Res. — D. Mehta
- Drug Reg. Affairs — J. Leader
- Dev. Planning — C. Harbert
- Dev. Res. — D. O'Shea

Pfizer Sales, Research Expenditures and Research Resources, 1950-1995

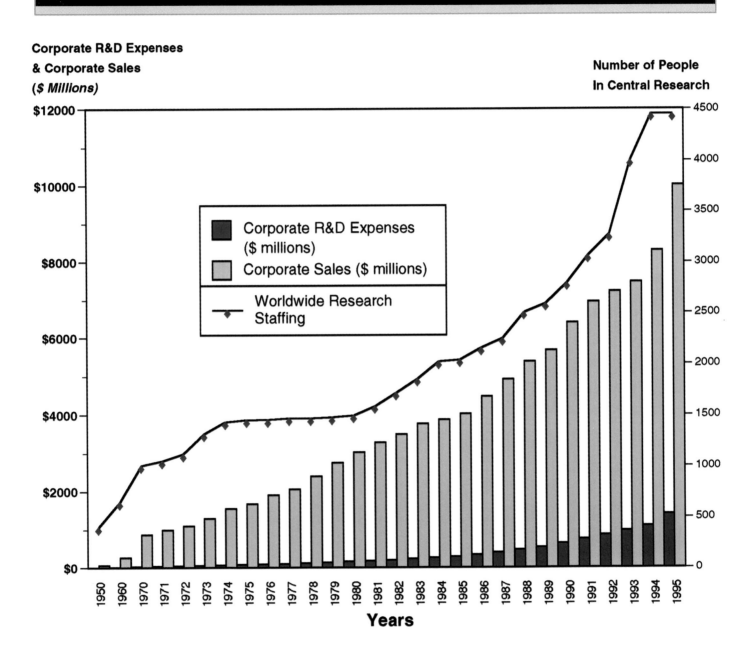

Corporate R&D Expenses & Corporate Sales ($ Millions)

Number of People In Central Research

Legend:
- Corporate R&D Expenses ($ millions)
- Corporate Sales ($ millions)
- Worldwide Research Staffing

Years

ACKNOWLEDGMENTS

Many people contributed to the writing of this history of Central Research. Ogden Tanner is the principal author who conducted all of the original interviews of key people and then produced the initial draft of the book based on those interviews. Particular thanks are due to the following people who were kind enough to read the early drafts in their entirety to check for accuracy of the historical facts: Barry Bloom, Lloyd Conover, Rex Pinson and George Milne. Sandra DiRoma served as proofreader and fact-checker and researched some graphics appearing in the appendix of the book. A number of Pfizer people reviewed and updated sections of the book relevant to their own experiences in Central Research. These reviewers included Mike Bright, Beryl Dominy, Greg Gardiner, Hans Hess, Dick Hinman, Karen Katen, Dilip Mehta, Alistair Monro, Dan O'Shea, Alan Proctor, Ken Richardson, Peter Ringrose, Steve Ryder, Craig Saxton, Karen Scappaticci, Ken Taksen, Dave Trecker, Manfred von Schach and Ian Williams.

Roger Burges and Rex Pinson were helpful in constructing some of the organizational charts shown in the appendix of the book. Elaine Bentley and Sandra DiRoma worked from a variety of sources to collect hundreds of pictures from Pfizer's past, from which the pictures in this book were selected.

Not surprisingly, in some cases the recollections of different people varied significantly about events that occurred up to 25 years ago. Where this happened, I attempted to reach a consensus by speaking to the key participants whenever possible. However, I'm sure there remain some historical events described in this book which remain controversial. We did the best we could in those situations, but factual records are often sparse and memories fade (or become distorted) over the decades.

Read this book to get the big picture of the history of Pfizer Central Research, and don't let the very few controversial details or inadvertent omissions get in the way. Read about some of the key players and events, the heartbreaks and the successes that are woven into the fabric that constitutes the history of Pfizer Central Research. The hope is that you will appreciate the roots from which this organization grew, in order to better understand where we came from and also to help you see the role you now play in helping us to get where we are going in the future.

J. G. LOMBARDINO
Coordinating Editor

January 1996

All bold listings indicate illustrated material.